Getting Started with Ionic

Get up and running with developing effective Hybrid
Mobile Apps with Ionic

Rahat Khanna

[PACKT] open source *
PUBLISHING   community experience distilled

BIRMINGHAM - MUMBAI

Getting Started with Ionic

First published: January 2016

Production reference: 2220116

Published by Packt Publishing Ltd.
Livery Place
35 Livery Street
Birmingham B3 2PB, UK.

ISBN 978-1-78439-057-0

www.packtpub.com

Credits

Author
Rahat Khanna

Reviewer
Nikola Brežnjak

Commissioning Editor
Dipika Gaonkar

Acquisition Editor
Aaron Lazar

Content Development Editor
Priyanka Mehta

Technical Editor
Dhiraj Chandanshive

Copy Editor
Joanna McMahon

Project Coordinator
Izzat Contractor

Proofreader
Safis Editing

Indexer
Rekha Nair

Production Coordinator
Manu Joseph

Cover Work
Manu Joseph

Foreword

This book is the result of four months of intensive writing and coding on the part of Rahat Khanna, a dedicated Ionic community member, experienced developer, and excellent writer. We were really happy to hear that Rahat was writing an Ionic book because we think very highly of his blog posts, which have also been very popular among members of our developer community.

The book is ideal for new Ionic developers who have some prior web development experience. The book contains code samples related to a single app that readers build as they move from chapter to chapter.

In the first few chapters, Rahat offers a solid conceptual base for Angular and for Hybrid Mobile App development in general. He teaches users how to set up a native development environment and use the Ionic command-line interface.

In later chapters, Rahat takes a deep dive into Ionic's architecture and different components. Experienced Ionic developers will appreciate his chapters on integrating backend services and mBaaS with Ionic apps.

In addition, the book touches upon Ionic Platform Services and Ionic 2's new features and migration path.

By the time they complete this book, readers will be able to build a mobile application with a native-looking user interface and interactions with device APIs and publish it to the app stores.

I began my career as a developer and built many internal Hybrid Apps for my company. I chose Ionic because it offered the only complete solution for Hybrid Mobile App development, which allows me to focus on development; whereas Ionic handled architecture and design. Ionic offers a complete ecosystem to build performant, beautiful mobile apps using a single code base, which saves organization's both money and time and allows them to leverage the existing skills of their web developers.

As a core team member of Ionic and Ionic's developer advocate, I travel around the U.S. to speak about Ionic and teach developers how to use it. I hope that you find this book to be a great introduction to Ionic and also a way to build upon your existing skills.

Mike Hartington
Providence, Rhode Island

About the Author

Rahat Khanna is a techno-nerd experienced in developing web and mobile apps for many international MNCs and start-ups. He has completed his Bachelors in Technology with Computer Science & Engineering as specialisation. During the past 7 years, he has worked for a multinational IT service company and ran his own entrepreneurial venture also in his early twenties. He has worked on ranging projects from static HTML websites to scalable web applications and engaging mobile apps. Along with his current job as a Senior UI developer at Flipkart, a billion dollar e-commerce firm, he now blogs on the latest technology frameworks on sites www.airpair.com, appsonmob.com, and so on and delivers talks at community events. He has been helping individual developers and startups in their Ionic projects to deliver amazing mobile apps.

I live in Bangalore, India with my wife Palak who has been instrumental in motivating me to share my knowledge with the world and write this book. Also, I would like to thank my parents and family to support me in my endeavours. I would also like to thank Packt Publishing and their entire team for helping constantly throughout the whole experience of finishing the book. Finally, I am also indebted to all my career mentors and colleagues especially Sunil Khokhar and Rahul Luthra who have helped me in constantly learning new things and growing as a professional.

About the Reviewer

Nikola Brežnjak is an engineer at heart and a jack-of-all-trades kind of guy. For those who care about titles, he has a master's degree in computing. For the past eight years, he worked in the betting software industry where he made use of his knowledge in areas ranging from full stack (web and desktop) development to game development through Linux and database administration and use of various languages (C#, PHP, JavaScript to name just a few). Recently, he's been interested in the Ionic Framework, and he likes to help out on StackOverflow where he is currently in the top 0.X%.

He self-published the book *Getting MEAN with MEMEs* via Leanpub, available at `https://leanpub.com/meantodo`. Also, he self-published the book about Ionic Framework via Leanpub, `https://leanpub.com/ionic-framework`. He was a technical reviewer for the book *Deploying Node.js*, *Sandro Pasquali*, as well as for the video *Beginning Ionic Hybrid Application Development*, *Troy Miles*, both by Packt Publishing. You can find out more about him through his blog at `http://www.nikola-breznjak.com/blog`.

He lives in Croatia with his lovely wife and daughter whom he would like to thank to support him in all his geeky endeavors. Also, he would like to thank his parents to teach him the power of hard and consistent work.

www.PacktPub.com

Support files, eBooks, discount offers, and more

For support files and downloads related to your book, please visit www.PacktPub.com.

Did you know that Packt offers eBook versions of every book published, with PDF and ePub files available? You can upgrade to the eBook version at www.PacktPub.com and as a print book customer, you are entitled to a discount on the eBook copy. Get in touch with us at service@packtpub.com for more details.

At www.PacktPub.com, you can also read a collection of free technical articles, sign up for a range of free newsletters and receive exclusive discounts and offers on Packt books and eBooks.

https://www2.packtpub.com/books/subscription/packtlib

Do you need instant solutions to your IT questions? PacktLib is Packt's online digital book library. Here, you can search, access, and read Packt's entire library of books.

Why subscribe?

- Fully searchable across every book published by Packt
- Copy and paste, print, and bookmark content
- On demand and accessible via a web browser

Free access for Packt account holders

If you have an account with Packt at www.PacktPub.com, you can use this to access PacktLib today and view 9 entirely free books. Simply use your login credentials for immediate access.

Table of Contents

Preface   **vii**

Chapter 1: All About Hybrid Mobile Apps and Ionic Framework   **1**

Introducing a Hybrid Mobile Application   **2**

Types of Hybrid Mobile Apps   3
WebView-based Hybrid Apps   3
Cross-compiled Hybrid Apps   3

Anatomy of a Hybrid Mobile App   4
Custom WebView   5
Native library   5
Native to JS Bridge   6

Using web technologies to develop for mobile   **6**

What is AngularJS?   **6**

Important concepts in AngularJS   7
Modules   7
Directives   8
Controllers   8
Services   9
Templates   10
Expressions   11
Filters   11

Why use Apache Cordova?   **11**

Introducing Ionic Framework   **12**

Summary   **12**

Chapter 2: Setting up the Environment the Right Way   13

Setting up Native Mobile development environments   14
For iOS   14
Installing and running simulators for testing   15
For Android   15
Download links   16
Setting the environment variables   16
For Windows   16
For Linux/Mac OS   17
Managing Android SDK and emulators   17
Alternative to Android emulators – Genymotion   18
Ionic development environment   18
Installing NodeJS   18
Basic npm commands   19
Installing Cordova CLI and Ionic CLI   19
Installation command for Cordova CLI   19
Basic Ionic CLI commands   20
Building a dummy app   22
Popular issues faced and solutions   24
Alternative to installation fuss – Ionic Playground   25
Using Ionic Framework with different Code Editors   25
Brackets   25
Sublime Text   26
Visual Studio   26
Summary   26

Chapter 3: Start Building Your First Ionic App   27

Starting a new project   28
Multiple ways to start a project   28
Method 1 – using CDN-hosted library files   28
Method 2 – using Ionic Creator to design a prototype and start a project   30
Method 3 – using Ionic CLI locally   32
The anatomy of Ionic Project   33
Project folder structure and important files   33
Main components   35
The index.html file   35
App.js and the root module   36
Simple content directives – ion-content and ion-pane   37
The Ionic starter template   38
The blank template   38
The tabs template   38
The sidemenu template   40

The maps template   41
E-commerce sample app – BookStore   **42**
    Features   42
    Architecture and design   42
Summary   **43**
Chapter 4: Navigation and Routing in an Ionic App   **45**
Introduction to Angular UI Router   **46**
    States and URLs   46
    Nested states and views   47
        Using the dot notation   47
        Using the parent property 48
        Using object-based states 48
        Views for nested views   48
        Ways to transition to a state 48
        Abstract state   49
    Multiple and named views   49
        View names – relative versus abstract 50
    State parameters   50
        Basic parameters   51
        Regex parameters   51
        Query parameters   51
    State events and resolve   52
        Resolve   53
Ionic header and footer   **53**
    The <ion-header-bar> directive   54
    The <ion-footer-bar> directive   54
Ionic Tabs   **55**
    The <ion-tabs> directive   55
    The <ion-tab> directive   56
Ionic side menu   **57**
    The <ion-side-menus> directive   57
    The <ion-side-menu> directive   57
    The <ion-side-menu-content> directive   58
    Other important directives   58
Navigation and back menus   **59**
Navigation and layout to be used in BookStore   **59**
Summary   **60**
Chapter 5: Accessorizing Your App with Ionic Components   **61**
Ionic CSS components   **62**
    Header   62
    Footer   63

Buttons	63
Icon buttons	64
Button bar	64
Lists	65
List dividers	65
List icons	65
List buttons	66
Item avatars or thumbnails	66
Cards	66
Forms	67
Input elements	67
Checkbox	68
Radio button list	68
Toggle	69
Range	69
Tabs	69
Grid	70
Utility	71
Ionic JS components	**71**
Actionsheet – $ionicActionSheet	72
Backdrop – $ionicBackdrop	73
Form inputs	73
The <ion-checkbox> directive	73
The <ion-radio> directive	74
The <ion-toggle> directive	74
Gestures and events	74
The $ionicGesture service	74
The on method	74
The off method	75
Gesture events	75
Lists	76
The <ion-list> directive	76
Loading – $ionicLoading	78
Modal – $ionicModal	79
The IonicModal controller	79
Popover – $ionicPopover	80
Spinner – ion-spinner	80
Miscellaneous components	**80**
$ionicPosition	80
$ionicConfigProvider	81
Summary	**81**

Chapter 6: Integrating App with Backend Services   83

$http services   84
  The response object   85
  The $http constructor method   85
Ionic services vs factories   86
  Ionic service – authentication service   86
  Ionic factory – BooksFactory   88
$resource and REST API   90
Demystifying mBaaS   91
Integrating with Parse   92
  Step 1 – creating an app on Parse   92
  Step 2 – getting API keys   93
  Step 3 – configuring appropriate settings   93
  Step 4 – integrating SDK or integrating using REST API   93
    Using SDK – downloading and overview   93
    Using REST API   94
Integrating to Firebase   94
Summary   95

Chapter 7: Testing App on Real Devices   97

Testing on browser emulators   98
  Overview of device mode in Chrome dev tools   98
Ionic view app   100
  The Ionic upload command   100
  Viewing your app   101
Making debug build   102
  Android debug build   102
  iOS debug build   103
Remote debugging   104
  Remote debugging using Chrome dev tools   104
  Android debugging   105
  iOS debugging   105
  Remote debugging using jsconsole.com   106
Testing using Ngrok   107
Summary   108

Chapter 8: Working with Cordova Plugins – ngCordova   109

Introduction to Cordova plugins   110
  Plugin management   111
Integrating ngCordova to Ionic App   111
Important plugins   112
  Camera plugin   112

Push Notifications	115
Geolocation	117
Contacts	119
Network	**120**
Device sensors	122
Device motion	122
Device orientation	123
Custom Cordova plugin development	**125**
Summary	**125**
Chapter 9: Future of Ionic	**127**
Ionic cloud services	**128**
Ionic Creator	128
Ionic Market	128
Ionic Push	129
Ionic Deploy	131
Using Ionic Deploy	132
Ionic Analytics	132
Ionic Package	133
Ionic Lab	133
Ionic v2	**134**
New features	134
Angular 2, ES6, and Typescript	134
Abstracted annotations	135
Material design	135
Enhanced Native Integration	135
Powerful Theming	135
Improved navigation and routing	135
Migration to v2	136
Summary	**136**
Index	**137**

Preface

Hybrid Mobile Apps have become a promising choice in mobile app development to achieve cost effectiveness and rapid development. Ionic has been instrumental in setting the benchmark in this space as it focuses on performance. It has evolved as the most popular choice for Hybrid Mobile App development as it tends to match the native experience and provides robust components/tools to build apps.

Getting Started with Ionic equips any web developer with the practical knowledge required to use modern web technologies in building amazing Hybrid Mobile Apps using Ionic. This fast-paced, practical book explains all the important concepts of AngularJS and Cordova framework required to develop Ionic apps. Then, it gives you a brief introduction to Hybrid Mobile Applications. It will guide you through setting up the development environment for different mobile platforms and through the multiple options and features available in Ionic, so you can use them in your mobile apps. Features, such as the side menu, tabs, touch interactions, and native features, such as bar code, camera, and geolocations, are all covered. Finally, we'll show you how to use Cordova plugins and use Ionic cloud services to empower your mobile apps.

What this book covers

Chapter 1, All About Hybrid Mobile Apps and Ionic Framework, covers the introduction to Hybrid Mobile Applications and the technologies used to develop these apps. This chapter will also include all important concepts regarding AngularJS and Apache Cordova, which readers need to know before building Ionic apps.

Chapter 2, Setting up the Environment the Right Way, covers setting up the native development environments for required platforms and then installing Ionic and required dependencies to start building Ionic apps. It will include details about Ionic command-line interface and the important features it provides for rapid development.

Chapter 3, *Start Building Your First Ionic App*, includes instructions for starting a new project and leveraging Ionic starter templates to bootstrap easily. It also covers the explanation about the design of the app structure and how you can plan to develop your app on top of it.

Chapter 4, *Navigation and Routing in an Ionic App*, covers how to create routes and layouts for navigation. It will teach the reader about views, Ionic header/footer sections, and different layout components, such as tabs, side menu, and modals. It also includes the basic routes and navigation setup for our sample app.

Chapter 5, *Accessorizing Your App with Ionic Components*, covers different components, which will be used in building the mobile app. It has two major categories: one is CSS components, which include grid framework and some reusable CSS classes to be used to design UI. The other category is Javascript components, which will facilitate building the business logic and UI interactions for the app.

Chapter 6, *Integrating App with Backend Services*, includes explanation about creating Ionic services and factories, which will interact with backend services. Ionic Apps can be integrated with all kinds of web services, REST APIs, SOAP services, and even cloud-based **mBaaS** (**Mobile Backend as a Services**) such as Parse and Firebase.

Chapter 7, *Testing App on Real Devices*, covers tools and techniques used to test and debug the app on your actual devices.

Chapter 8, *Working with Cordova Plugins - ngCordova*, teaches the reader how to use ready-made Cordova plugins, which help the mobile app to talk to native device APIs, such as sensors, camera, and geolocation. It will also explain how to integrate an open source Angular wrapper named ngCordova for cordova plugins into an Ionic App.

Chapter 9, *Future of Ionic*, includes an introduction to various cloud Ionic services available online under the Ionic.io platform. It also covers about the future of Ionic v2 along with Angular v2 talking about new features and migration path.

What you need for this book

For this book, you require a system with Windows, Mac, or Linux OS. You need to install NodeJS and NPM to manage dependencies for different projects. This book will guide you through the setup for mobile app development platforms for iOS and Android. Test devices having Android and iOS would be required to test the mobile apps.

Who this book is for

This book is ideal for any web developer who wants to enter into the world of mobile app development but has no clue where to start. Ionic is an ideal starting point and provides a smooth learning curve to help you build Hybrid Apps using web technologies and to develop native apps for iOS and Android; you do not need to know multiple languages. This book will also be useful for Hybrid App developers who have not found the perfect framework to ensure that users get a rich experience from your apps.

Conventions

In this book, you will find a number of text styles that distinguish between different kinds of information. Here are some examples of these styles and an explanation of their meaning.

Code words in text, database table names, folder names, filenames, file extensions, pathnames, dummy URLs, code tags, user input, and Twitter handles are shown in bold.

A block of code is set as follows:

```
<ion-nav-bar class="bar-stable">
  <ion-nav-back-button>
  </ion-nav-back-button>
</ion-nav-bar>
<ion-nav-view></ion-nav-view>
```

When we wish to draw your attention to a particular part of a code block, the relevant lines or items are set in bold:

```
<ion-nav-bar class="bar-stable">
  <ion-nav-back-button>
  </ion-nav-back-button>
</ion-nav-bar>
<ion-nav-view></ion-nav-view>
```

Any command-line input or output is written as follows:

```
$ ionic start MenuDemo sidemenu
```

New terms and **important words** are shown in bold. Words that you see on the screen, for example, in menus or dialog boxes, appear in the text like this: "In order to run an app on an Android device, enable **Developer Options** and check the **USB Debugging** option from the settings."

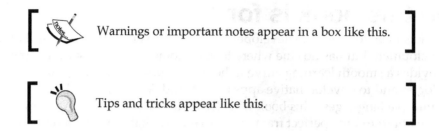

Warnings or important notes appear in a box like this.

Tips and tricks appear like this.

Reader feedback

Feedback from our readers is always welcome. Let us know what you think about this book—what you liked or disliked. Reader feedback is important for us as it helps us develop titles that you will really get the most out of.

To send us general feedback, simply e-mail feedback@packtpub.com, and mention the book's title in the subject of your message.

If there is a topic that you have expertise in and you are interested in either writing or contributing to a book, see our author guide at www.packtpub.com/authors.

Customer support

Now that you are the proud owner of a Packt book, we have a number of things to help you to get the most from your purchase.

Downloading the example code

You can download the example code files from your account at http://www.packtpub.com for all the Packt Publishing books you have purchased. If you purchased this book elsewhere, you can visit http://www.packtpub.com/support and register to have the files e-mailed directly to you.

Running the example code

The example codes available on the website are taken from Ionic Projects. In order to run them successfully on your machines, you need to create an empty Ionic Project and then copy the example code files to the www folder of your Ionic Project and then run npm install first and then ionic serve command to run locally or ionic run [android|ios] to run on the device.

Downloading the color images of this book

We also provide you with a PDF file that has color images of the screenshots/ diagrams used in this book. The color images will help you better understand the changes in the output. You can download this file from `http://www.packtpub.com/ sites/default/files/downloads/0570OS_ColorImages.pdf`.

Errata

Although we have taken every care to ensure the accuracy of our content, mistakes do happen. If you find a mistake in one of our books—maybe a mistake in the text or the code—we would be grateful if you could report this to us. By doing so, you can save other readers from frustration and help us improve subsequent versions of this book. If you find any errata, please report them by visiting `http://www.packtpub. com/submit-errata`, selecting your book, clicking on the **Errata Submission Form** link, and entering the details of your errata. Once your errata are verified, your submission will be accepted and the errata will be uploaded to our website or added to any list of existing errata under the Errata section of that title.

To view the previously submitted errata, go to `https://www.packtpub.com/books/ content/support` and enter the name of the book in the search field. The required information will appear under the **Errata** section.

Piracy

Piracy of copyrighted material on the Internet is an ongoing problem across all media. At Packt, we take the protection of our copyright and licenses very seriously. If you come across any illegal copies of our works in any form on the Internet, please provide us with the location address or website name immediately so that we can pursue a remedy.

Please contact us at `copyright@packtpub.com` with a link to the suspected pirated material.

We appreciate your help in protecting our authors and our ability to bring you valuable content.

Questions

If you have a problem with any aspect of this book, you can contact us at `questions@packtpub.com`, and we will do our best to address the problem.

1
All About Hybrid Mobile Apps and Ionic Framework

In this chapter, we are going to learn what a Hybrid Mobile Application is and the current technology ecosystems supporting it. We will also be introduced to Ionic Framework and the reasons that should lead you to decide on Ionic as your preferred choice. The topics covered in this chapter will be as follows:

- Introduction to a Hybrid Mobile Application
- Using web technologies to develop for mobile devices
- What is AngularJS?
- Why use Apache Cordova?
- Introducing Ionic Framework

The term 'website' has become a word of the past. 'App' is the new buzzword, and the world is moving away from old software systems to new jazzy apps. App, or application in terms of a software, is a more sophisticated system, which involves enabling a lot more features to the user rather than just providing static information like a traditional website.

Web apps have a lot of limitations such as requiring Internet connectivity all the time and restrictions on fully utilizing the hardware capabilities of the device on which you are accessing them. Mobile apps, on the other hand, defy all of these limitations and provide an engaging user experience.

Mobiles have emerged as the most popular channel for user engagement. The number of smartphone users is expected to grow to nearly 2.16 billion in 2016 (`http://www.emarketer.com/Article/2-Billion-Consumers-Worldwide-Smartphones-by-2016/1011694`), which is more than one quarter of the global population. The growth rate of smartphone usage has been tremendous and is expected to grow day by day.

Mobile adoption is associated with some of the following trivial points:

- Mobiles are the only device that we keep with us the whole day
- Kids (between the ages of two and five) know more about using a smartphone than tieing their shoelaces
- Time spent on mobile phones is increasing 14 times faster than time spent on desktop media
- People check their smartphones first thing when they wake up instead of wishing good morning to their partners or family

After reading through these points, one must think that the perfect mobile strategy has become a necessity for every business. Going mobile is not a choice any more, rather everyone has to decide which way to go: mobile-first, mobile-only, or mobile-after. If you are a new start-up, an existing enterprise, or an individual developer, Native Mobile apps have a steep learning curve and high development costs for covering all platforms. Mobile ecosystems have become fragmented with multiple OSs such as iOS, Android, Windows, and numerous OEMs such as Samsung, LG, HTC, and others. A Hybrid Mobile Application, about which you will learn in this chapter, is the perfect savior for you. Ionic Framework is a popular hybrid app development framework that helps us in creating Native-looking Apps for multiple platforms using a single codebase.

Introducing a Hybrid Mobile Application

A common misconception is that a Hybrid Mobile Application cannot be installed on the device, but that is wrong. A Hybrid Mobile App is like any other Native Mobile App, which can be installed on devices and published using App stores. They can access the device hardware such as camera, accelerometer, GPS, and so on.

As we have discussed, there are multiple mobile platforms such as iOS, Android, Windows, plus many new ones such as Firefox OS and Tizen that have emerged lately. The development environment and programming languages are different for each of these. We have to code using Objective-C for iOS apps, Java (Android SDK) for Android apps, C#/VB.net with XAML for Windows Phone apps. If any entity requires its mobile presence across all these platforms, multiple teams and different codebases need to be maintained, which is too cumbersome.

Hybrid Mobile Apps can be developed for multiple platforms using a single codebase. However, some specialized code needs to be written for each platform to harness the native APIs for it.

Types of Hybrid Mobile Apps

There are broadly two categories of Hybrid Mobile Apps in the industry:

- WebView-based Hybrid Apps
- Cross-compiled Hybrid Apps

WebView-based Hybrid Apps

Each native mobile platform has a common control/component called a WebView, which is nothing but a Chromeless browser. This component is utilized to open locally hosted web content, for example, HTML pages, CSS files, and JavaScript code. HTML5 and CSS3 provide capabilities to develop responsive apps, which can render nicely on multiple screen sizes. The web technologies have evolved to handle the touch interactions that make them a perfect candidate for developing solutions for smartphones and tablets. The example of development platform and frameworks using this approach are Cordova, Ionic Framework, KendoUI Mobile, F7, Mobile Angular UI, Onsen UI, and many more.

Cross-compiled Hybrid Apps

Another category of hybrid app involves cross-compiling multiple native apps from a single programming language. For example, the developer will code using a single language, say, A, which can be converted at compile time or run time into native language components. Generally, these types of frameworks and platforms leverage creating a bridge or a mapping of native components to their custom constructs in the programming language intended for development. Examples for this category are Xamarin (C#), Kony (JS), Corona (C Lang.), Qt(C++), and many more.

We will be talking about WebView-based Hybrid Apps in this book as they are more suitable for large-scale and complex Mobile Apps. In this next section, we will learn more about the anatomy of Hybrid Apps and how they are capable of developing Native Apps for multiple platforms.

Anatomy of a Hybrid Mobile App

Hybrid Apps are no different from Native Mobile Apps that are installed on any mobile platform such as Android or iOS. On any platform, the core device APIs for hardware such as GPS, Camera, Accelerometer, and so on will be exposed by the Mobile OS. The following diagram shows the anatomy of Hybrid Mobile App:

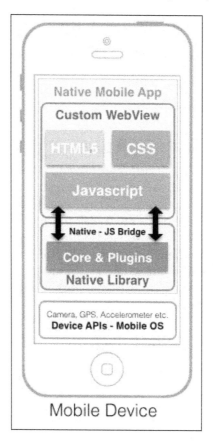

These APIs are consumed by the native code of your Hybrid Apps. All the components of Hybrid Apps are discussed in detail in the following section.

Custom WebView

Each native platform development kit has a component called WebView, which is nothing but a Chromeless browser control. WebView has the capability to open local or remote web content, which is exploited by Hybrid App frameworks to display the UI of the app using web technologies. This is the most important component of a Hybrid App and has a significant role in deciding the performance of the app.

WebViews in popular platforms such as iOS and Android used to have a different rendering engine and JavaScript engine than the latest browser (Chrome or Safari). Last year, Apple released a new control in its SDK called WKWebView, which uses all the performance optimization such as the Nitro JavaScript engine used by the Safari browser on iOS. On similar lines, Google also released an updated WebView, which uses the rendering engine and JavaScript runtime of Chromium (Chrome browser). Google has also launched a new feature called Updatable WebView from Android (5.0) Lollipop, which enables you to upgrade only the WebView of your Hybrid App.

Crosswalk is an interesting open source project that enables app developers to embed custom WebView into your Hybrid App. With these advancements, Hybrid Apps have become capable of using the latest web features such as WebRTC for real-time multimedia communication, and WebGL for advanced graphics rendering.

Native library

All the Hybrid App development frameworks based on WebView have their own native library. It comprises some basic utility functions that support the Hybrid App such as creating app configs, bootstrap code for Native Apps, customization for the WebView, common error/exception handling logic, and so on. The native library is specific to the mobile platform as it involves interacting with the core OS APIs and components.

The most popular framework, for example, Apache Cordova/Phonegap has an architecture of dividing its native library into a core section and pluggable components called plugins. This helps in reducing the bare minimum size of a Hybrid App. Developers can use only the plugins they require for a specific app. A plugin will include native code for a particular feature and a JavaScript interface exposing the native functionality. For example, if you want to use the Fingerprint Authentication API for iOS, you can just include the plugin for iOS and use it apart from the core. It also enables communities to contribute by developing open source plugins.

Native to JS Bridge

In a WebView-based Hybrid App, the UI is always written using web technologies, and JavaScript is the language for writing logic and hence we need to call our native code from JS and get results to JS also. A bridge has two functions, one is to enable JS to call any native method and the other is to allow native methods to execute callbacks in JS. The bridge comprises different implementations in different platforms to call JS from native. For example, in Android, Java objects are marshalled into the WebView and can be called from the JS. In iOS, JS calls a specific URL scheme, which is interpreted by the native code. The reverse bridge is a simple global JS function that is called by the WebView passing special arguments such as callback results or specific commands.

Using web technologies to develop for mobile

After understanding what is happening inside a Hybrid App, it is important to know how web technologies are used to develop Mobile Apps. We can use simple HTML5, CSS, and JS to create mobile-specific UIs and enable them to be viewed in the WebView discussed previously. But any website, even if it is a mobile web app, should not be directly packaged into a Hybrid App. This is the most popular mistake developers make and then complain about the performance of the Hybrid App.

A Hybrid Mobile App UI needs to have proper separation of concerns and can be best developed using **single page architecture (SPA)** or MV* architecture. It helps in providing a seamless user experience and provide a Native App such as engagement. It also equips developers with segregated areas to code, for example, writing views using HTML5 markup templates, styling using CSS, and logic in JS.

Ionic Framework uses an open source MV* framework called AngularJS to build robust Native-looking Hybrid Mobile Apps. AngularJS is an extensive topic that cannot be covered here, but we will learn about some basics that are essential in utilizing Ionic Framework to its full potential.

What is AngularJS?

AngularJS is a JavaScript-based MV* framework that provides a strong backbone to scalable and complex web apps. It also enables developers to extend HTML and program their apps in a declarative paradigm in lieu of an imperative programming style. AngularJS provides us with a way of creating reusable components, setting standard templates in HTML, and reusable business logic with the ability to bind data dynamically to it.

AngularJS is a perfect fit for creating rich Mobile UI Apps as it provides a robust structure to the frontend, which is a reason why the Ionic team has chosen it as their core.

Important concepts in AngularJS

In order to build apps using AngularJS we need to understand the core concepts used in AngularJS and learn how to use them. The prerequisite for learning AngularJS is decent knowledge of HTML, CSS, and JavaScript. The core concepts that will be discussed include modules, directives, controllers, expressions, and filters.

Modules

In AngularJS, modules are at the core of everything because an AngularJS App is defined as a module itself. A module is a container for different sections of the app such as controllers, directives, services, and so on. A module can have other module dependencies injected at run time. This feature of AngularJS is called **DI (Dependency Injection)**. It provides super flexibility for unit testing as dependencies can be mocked and injected.

Each module has two important lifecycle hooks implemented as methods registering callbacks. The methods are config and run. The config method is used to set up or provide important configuration settings such as routes, states, and so on, whereas the run function is used like the main method for initiating the module inside the callback registered:

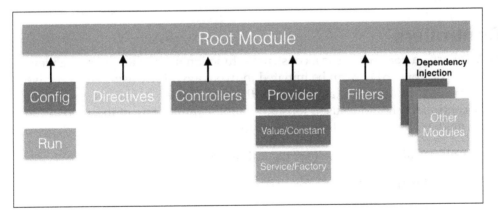

Directives

Directives are the most important and yet the most complex part of AngularJS. They can be easily described as a set of markers on DOM elements such as element name, CSS class, an attribute, or a comment, which lets the AngularJS compiler know that specified behavior needs to be attached there. It is advised to encapsulate any DOM manipulation logic into a directive while developing an AngularJS App.

There are plenty of in-built core directives that are part of the `ng-module` and used in each angular app. We will discuss the essential ones in order to understand the functioning of a directive.

`ng-app` is the core directive that bootstraps our app. The root angular module name needs to be passed to this directive and is generally used as an attribute, for example:

```
<html ng-app="my-app">
```

`ng-model` is a directive used for binding models from controllers to the views. We will learn about the scope in the text ahead, which is used to hold the models as Plain Old JavaScript Objects. `ng-model` is used with input, select, and text area controls, for example:

```
<input type='text' name='textField' ng-model="my-var">
```

There are many other directives such as `ng-class`, `ng-show`, `ng-hide`, and so on, which you will use while developing your app. Ionic Framework has built most of its components as custom directives and will be used frequently to develop Hybrid Apps using the framework.

Controllers

In AngularJS, a `controller` is a constructor function used to augment the view models. The `controller` can be initiated in two ways, either using the directive `ng-controller` or it can be associated with a route/state. According to Angular docs, controllers should be used for setting up the initial state of the `$scope` (view model) object and adding behavior to it.

We should refrain from using it for the following logic:

- DOM manipulations
- Formatting input
- Input validations
- Sharing of data should be done using services

The example code for a basic controller is:

```
var newApp = angular.module('NewApp',[]);
newApp.controller('FirstController',['$scope',function($scope) {
  $scope.modelObj = { name:'MyDummyObject' };
  $scope.updateName = function(newName) {
    $scope.modelObj.name = newName;
  }
});
```

 We define the dependency injection twice, first as a string and then as an argument to avoid problems during the minification of your JS files. Read more details at https://docs.angularjs.org/guide/di.

Services

In AngularJS, services are used to store business logic and organize your code into logical units or entities. Angular services are lazily loaded and are wired together using Dependency Injection, as discussed earlier. AngularJS services are singletons and thus instantiated only the first time they are encountered as a dependency to any controller or module.

AngularJS has multiple built-in services out of which $http is the most important one. The $http service provides a wrapper on the browser's XMLHTTPRequest object, or more popularly known as Ajax requests.

We can create AngularJS services using two module factory methods. The methods used are .service or .factory. The former is used when we create the service instance using a constructor function, and the latter is used when a factory function returns the instance of the service. Conceptually, we should use .service when we are integrating to any external API and use .factory if we are creating objects representing app models.

The code sample to create services using both methods is given as follows:

```
// Using Factory Method
var newApp = angular.module('NewApp',[]);
newApp.factory('MyService',[function() {
  var serviceInstance = {};
  var privateMethod = function() { return 'result'; };
  serviceInstance.exposedMethod = function() {
    return privateMethod();
  };
  return serviceInstance;
});
```

In the given code, a factory function available on the `angular.module` object is used to return a service instance that contains public methods. The service can encapsulate private methods to include logic that should not be exposed:

```
// Using Service Method
var newApp = angular.module('NewApp',[]);
newApp.service('MyService',[function() {
  var privateMethod = function() { return 'result'; };
  this.exposedMethod = function() {
    return privateMethod();
  };
});
```

Services in Angular can be used in the following ways:

- Representing business entities/models
- Sharing data across controllers
- Interface to external web service calls or Ajax requests

Templates

In AngularJS, templates are associated with a route/state to display HTML elements and Angular-specific elements. Template code can be directly passed in JS or TemplateURL, for example, URL to the template file can be passed to any object. Angular combines the template to the controller and models to display dynamic content to the user on the browser. $scope is used to bind the controller to the template.

Templates can use Angular directives and expressions that are compiled by the $compile service. The following code shows a simple Angular template:

```
<html ng-app>
  <head>
    <title>My First Angular Template</title>
  </head>
  <body>
    <h1>Main Section</h1>
    <div ng-controller='MyCtrl'>
      <p>{{ contentStr }}</p>
      <p>Date : {{ dateStr | dateFormat }}</p>
    </div>
    Name: <input type='text' ng-model='name'>
  </body>
</html>
```

Expressions

Expressions are code snippets put in AngularJS templates to create bindings between controllers and templates. The expressions are, by default, represented by {{ }} in the templates. Angular expressions are different from JavaScript expressions as they have some restrictions. They can contain basic arithmetic or concatenation operations, but no control flow statement or function declarations. Angular expressions run against the context of the scope, for example, variables in the bindings are evaluated on the scope object for each respective controller.

Filters

Filters are used in expressions to format data before displaying it. Filters are applied using the | operator. There are in-built filters such as currency, number, date, lowercase, and so on.

Example of expressions with a filter in a template:

```
<p> Total : {{ amount * 32 | currency }} </p>
```

amount is a scope model, using the * arithmetic operator and the currency filter.

Why use Apache Cordova?

Apache Cordova is a WebView-based Hybrid App development framework used to build cross-platform Native Apps. It is one of the most popular frameworks that has been open sourced by Adobe and is maintained by the Apache Foundation. Adobe maintains another branch with added features named Phonegap. They also have a cloud-based service called Phonegap Build (http://build.phonegap.com), which generates the native builds on the fly so that you do not need to install native SDKs.

It follows the same architecture discussed previously, having a minimal core and ability to add plugins for extra functionality to your app. Apache Cordova has a high number of open source plugins that provide excellent capability to Hybrid Apps. Any developer can also create a custom plugin to expose unique native functionality in a Hybrid App. It also consists of a CLI interface to provide commands for managing plugins and automating builds for multiple platforms. Apache Cordova is a widely tested and accepted framework and is recommended for building Hybrid Mobile Apps from web content.

Introducing Ionic Framework

Ionic Framework is a Hybrid App development framework that enables developers to build Native-looking Mobile Apps using web technologies (HTML5, CSS3, and JS). Ionic Framework is completely open source so that developers can build and publish their apps to the marketplace without any cost.

Ionic is built on top of the AngularJS framework and uses Apache Cordova for building apps from web content. Ionic Framework includes a set of amazing Angular directives that makes it very easy to develop for mobile. For example, ListView, Optimized Touch gestures, Side Menus, Popup, Tabs, and mobile-specific input elements.

Ionic has ready-made UI for mobile components, which helps in rapid application development for Hybrid Mobile Apps. Ionic has native-looking stylesheets for Android and iOS, which automatically get applied based on the platform build.

Ionic Framework has evolved into an ecosystem with a suite of mobile development tools along with the framework itself. Ionic CLI has amazing options such as Ionic Lab and Live Reload, which helps developers save lot of development time. Ionic view is a Native App for iOS and Android where developers can deploy and test their apps on the fly without packaging. Ionic.io is a complete cloud-based backend service platform where developers can manage their app data, view analytics, and manage push notifications from a single console.

Summary

We have learnt all about Hybrid Mobile Applications and how easy it is for a web developer to start building Mobile Apps using Ionic Framework. The concepts mentioned in this chapter will suffice in building apps using AngularJS, Cordova, and Ionic. In the coming chapters, we will build amazing Hybrid Mobile Apps that can be deployed to public app stores. In the next chapter we will learn about setting up the development environment and starting an initial project to bootstrap our development journey.

2
Setting up the Environment the Right Way

In this chapter we will learn how to set up our development environment and build a dummy app to verify the correct setup. This chapter also defines the possible and popular issues faced during setup so that you do not face any bottlenecks during the process. The instructions are separated for Windows OS, generic Linux OS, and Mac OS.

As we have discussed, Ionic has evolved into an ecosystem from a basic framework. It is very important that we set up our development tools the right way to leverage the full potential of this ecosystem.

We will be setting up a lot of software just for developing Mobile Apps, but if we want to use the power of developing for multiple platform apps using a single codebase, we have to do this. Any Native App is always built using the Native Development tools and hence we have to install and set up a Native Mobile development environment for all the platforms.

Apart from the build tools of native environments, a dev environment should provide ease of use and speed to the developer. Installing Ionic CLI based on NodeJS and Cordova would provide the extensive power of bootstrapping Ionic Projects with starter templates, managing Cordova plugins, and other dependencies. Code Editor should provide the developer with complete support for the programming languages an app is being built in. We will learn about some popular Code Editors that gel with Ionic App development. We will also build a dummy app to gain confidence of starting the actual development.

The following topics will be covered in this chapter:

- Setting up Native Mobile development environments:
    - For iOS
    - For Android
    - For Windows phone
- Ionic Development Environments:
    - Installing NodeJS
    - Installing Cordova and Ionic CLI
- Basic commands in Ionic CLI
- Building a dummy app
- Popular issues faced and solutions
- An alternative to the installation fuss — Ionic Play
- Using Ionic with different Code Editors:
    - Brackets
    - Sublime Text
    - Visual Studio

Setting up Native Mobile development environments

Native Mobile development environments are specific to your operating system and hence there will be separate instructions for installing on Windows/Mac/Linux. The native environment SDKs are heavy so would require fast Internet speed to download. You need to be on a good network to be able to download it.

For iOS

These days iOS Apps are built for iPhone, iPad and iWatch devices. Objective-C is the primary language used to develop iOS Native Apps. Xcode is Apple's **IDE** (**integrated development environment**), which includes a graphical user interface and many other features. iOS SDK is required along with Xcode as it provides additional tools, compilers, and frameworks to build iOS Apps for phones, tablets, and smartwear devices (iWatch).

For developing or building iOS Apps, a Macintosh machine is strictly required so if you do not have a Mac, please skip this section. Mac machines should have OS X 10.9.4 or later.

In order to download the latest version of Xcode and iOS SDK (bundled) for free, please follow these steps:

1. Go to the **Apple App Store** on your Mac (search for it or open from the dock).
2. Search for Xcode software to download in the top-right corner search box.
3. Click on the **Free** button to download it.

The website link for downloading Xcode is `https://developer.apple.com/xcode/`.

Xcode will be downloaded and installed in the `Applications` folder of your Mac machine.

Installing and running simulators for testing

In order to test our iOS apps, we either require a physical device or we can test it on a simulator. By default, the simulators are present in the Xcode. In order to install different iOS simulators for specific OS versions, please go to `https://developer.apple.com/ios/download/`.

To run the simulator, open Xcode, right click on the Xcode icon in the dock and go to **Open Developer Tools | iOS Simulator**. It will open an iOS device such as an iPad or iPhone, which can be changed by going to the top menu option **Hardware | Device | Specific Device**.

For Android

Android Apps are developed using a Java programming language so installing a Java environment is a requirement for it. Please download the latest JDK 7 (JRE would not work) from `http://www.oracle.com/technetwork/java/javase/downloads/index.html`. It is required to set the `PATH` and `JAVA_HOME` variable to refer to Java and javac binaries (we explain later how to do it).

Apache Ant is a Java build system used by Cordova/Ionic and Android SDK. In order to install Ant properly, download the binary from the link `http://ant.apache.org/bindownload.cgi` and follow these steps:

1. Move the downloaded file to a new location/folder for Ant.
2. Unpack the zip file where you want Ant to be installed.
3. Set the `PATH` variable and `ANT_HOME` to this directory.

Android SDK is available in two variants, one is a standalone SDK and the other is bundled with Code Editor Eclipse or indigenous Android Studio. There are separate binaries for Windows, Linux, and Mac OS. It is recommended to download and set up the standalone SDK for developing Hybrid Apps unless you want to try out native Android development too. We will be discussing setting up the standalone Android SDK only.

Download links

The following are some downloading links:

- Standalone SDK (recommended) [for all OSes]: `https://developer.android.com/sdk/installing/index.html?pkg=tools`

- Android Studio bundle [for all OSes]: `https://developer.android.com/tools/studio/index.html`

- Eclipse and ADT bundle [for all OSes]: `http://developer.android.com/sdk/installing/installing-adt.html`

Setting the environment variables

For Cordova command-line tools to work, or the CLI that is based upon them, you need to include the SDK's tools and platform-tools directories in your `PATH`.

For Windows

The following are the steps to set up Native Mobile development environments on Windows:

1. Click on the **Start** menu, right-click on **Computer**, and then select **Properties**.
2. Select **Advanced system settings** from the column on the left.
3. Select the **Environment Variables | PATH** variable and click **Edit**.

4. Append the path with a path to the platform tools and tools folder of SDK.

For example,`C:\Development\adt-bundle\sdk\platform-tools;C:\`
`Development\adt-bundle\sdk\tools`

For Linux/Mac OS

On a Mac you can use a text editor and on a Linux you can use vi editor to create/modify the `~/.bash_profile` file, adding a line such as the following, depending on where the SDK installs:

```
$ export PATH=${PATH}:/Development/adt-bundle/sdk/platform-tools:/
Development/adt-bundle/sdk/tools
```

Add the paths for Java and Ant if needed. This line in `~/.bash_profile` exposes these tools in newly opened terminal windows. If your terminal window is already open in OS X, or to avoid a logout/login on Linux, run this to make them available in the current terminal window:

```
$ source ~/.bash_profile
```

Managing Android SDK and emulators

Android has a large fragmentation in the OS versions being used and has different SDK packages for various versions. In the SDK tools, there is an SDK manager that helps to manage different SDK API versions. In order to manage SDK Manager, open `SDK Manager.exe` in Windows, whereas on a Mac/Linux open a terminal and navigate to the `/tools` directory in the location where the Android SDK is installed, then execute `android sdk`.

In Android, to test your apps, install it on an actual physical device or create a new emulator/virtual device using the SDK tools. These next steps should be followed:

1. Open the command prompt in Windows and terminal in Linux/Mac.

2. Go to the location where Android SDK is installed under the `tools` folder.

3. Execute the command `$ android avd` to open the **Virtual Device/Emulator Manager**.

Alternative to Android emulators – Genymotion

Android emulators are known to be slow and sloppy. If you want to debug or test your apps on emulators, use the Genymotion emulator as it is faster than the Android emulators. Apart from being fast, it has 20 mobile devices preconfigured to emulate. The Genymotion emulator uses VirtualBox, so install the latest version and then install Genymotion. The link to the Genymotion website is `https://www.genymotion.com/`.

Ionic development environment

Ionic Framework is based on Apache Cordova, which takes care of build and plugin management. Apache Cordova CLI uses the NodeJS package manager called NPM for dependency management.

Installing NodeJS

NodeJS is a JavaScript-based server-side environment to build backend systems. NodeJS has an efficient package manager that takes care of installing and maintaining a central repository of packages, version management, and dependency management. NPM has become the default dependency manager for a lot of other frameworks apart from NodeJS. Ionic Framework also leveraged this successful package manager so we have to install it for Hybrid App development.

In order to install NodeJS, download the binary for the respective OS—Windows, Linux, or Mac OS from `https://nodejs.org/download/`.

On a Mac or Linux, you can use a package manager such as brew to install NodeJS:

```
$ brew install node
```

After the node installation is complete, please type in the following commands to test the installation:

```
$ node -v
$ npm -v
```

The appropriate installed version for node and npm will be written to the output.

There is a `config.json` file generated that stores the dependent modules and meta information about the specific NodeJS project.

Basic npm commands

In order to install any npm package, the `install` command is used. It has an optional flag `-g` for installing any package globally so that it is accessible from anywhere. All the CLI packages such as Cordova CLI and Ionic CLI will be installed using these commands only. In order to update a package, run the second command:

```
$ npm install -g <package_name>
$ npm update -g <package_name>
```

Installing Cordova CLI and Ionic CLI

Cordova will be installed using the npm utility discussed previously. The Cordova CLI includes a set of scripts to automate the Cordova build process for wrapping of web content into Native Mobile Apps. It also includes commands to manage plugins. As discussed in *Chapter 1, All About Hybrid Mobile Apps and Ionic Framework*, Cordova is based on an architecture where the core library is included by default, but extra functionality needs to be utilized using plugins.

Installation command for Cordova CLI

In order to install Cordova, use the npm global `install` command as follows:

- **On a Mac/Linux machine**: `$ npm install -g cordova`
- **On a Windows machine**: `C:\>npm install -g cordova`

Cordova installation can be confirmed by checking the version of the installed package as follows:

```
$ cordova -v
```

The Ionic command-line interface provides an easy-to-use interface to perform basic functions such as creating an app, adding a platform, and building apps. It also provides commands to use Ionic platform services helping in rapid development of Hybrid Apps. Ionic CLI is installed in a method similar to Cordova with the following commands:

- **On a Mac/Linux machine**: `$ npm install -g ionic`
- **On a Windows machine**: `C:\>npm install -g ionic`

Ionic CLI extends the Cordova CLI and hence most of the Cordova commands need not be run directly. They can be run using the `ionic` keyword, where internally the Cordova package will be used. You can also view a list of exhaustive Ionic commands by executing `ionic help`.

Basic Ionic CLI commands

Ionic commands help you smoothly create a new project and test it easily while you are developing it. The first command you should learn to execute is the `ionic info` command. This would help you to know all about your system environment that you have set up so far. If there are any errors, you can debug and resolve them before beginning the development.

The command and a sample output is given here:

```
$ ionic info
Your system information:
OS: Mac OS X Yosemite
Node Version: v0.12.4
Cordova CLI: 5.1.1
Ionic CLI Version: 1.6.2
Xcode version: Xcode 6.4 Build version 6E35b
ios-sim version: 3.1.1
ios-deploy version: 1.7.0
```

Another quick utility command is to go to the Ionic docs for a specific topic:

```
$ ionic docs <TOPIC>
```

Please go through the commands in this section in order to understand the steps required to build a dummy app to test the environment.

The next command to learn is to start a new project. Ionic has multiple flags/options along with this command to set up your project initially. The main command is as follows:

```
$ ionic start [OPTIONS] <PATH> [template]
```

The options are many, including `-appname` to set the name, `--no-cordova` to create a structure without Cordova (for cloud builds such as a phonegap build service), `--template` for selecting the initial template, and so on.

If you want to preview your app in a browser during the development phase, this is the most important command for it. It has a handful of useful options for setting a port number, opening a specific browser, printing console logs, and so on:

```
$ ionic serve [OPTIONS]
```

In order to add a platform, please run the following command:

```
$ ionic platform [OPTIONS] <PLATFORM>
```

After adding the platforms we want to build, we can run our app on an actual connected device using this command:

```
$ ionic run [OPTIONS] <PLATFORM>
```

 In order to run an app on an Android device, enable **Developer Options** and check the **USB Debugging** option in the settings. More info is available at `http://developer.android.com/tools/device.html`.

We can make the app build for all the platforms in one go or a specific platform by mentioning its name in the following command. It builds the apps locally using the native SDK tools:

```
$ ionic build [OPTIONS] <PLATFORM>
```

Hybrid App development relies on the web view or the browser in the native SDK of the platform. Ionic provides a way to change the browser of a specific app, for example, using the crosswalk browser. There is a command to list the available browsers:

```
$ ionic browser list
```

Add a new browser for any platform and also have the ability to revert back:

```
$ ionic browser add crosswalk
$ ionic browser revert <PLATFORM>
```

Or else you can use the following command:

```
$ ionic browser rm crosswalk
```

Ionic provides a way to list and manage extra add-ons or browser packages to your app using the Ionic CLI, which we will learn in future chapters.

Building a dummy app

After successfully setting up the environment correctly, you must be excited to build your first app. In this section of the chapter, we will use the commands to learn how to create a sample Ionic-based Hybrid App and build it to run on an actual device or emulator:

1. We will create the initial project using the Ionic `start` command and name our project `MyFirstApp`. The output will be as illustrated in the following screenshot:

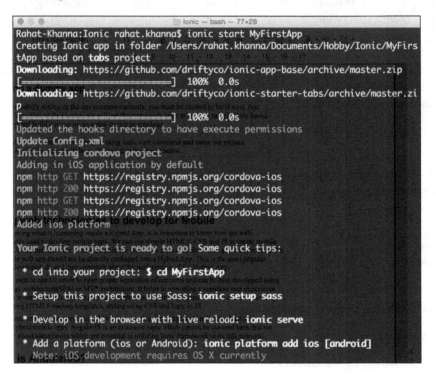

2. After the successful creation of your project with the default Ionic template, go to your project folder using the command `$ cd MyFirstApp`.

   Now, as we are in an Ionic `project` folder, we can run Ionic project-specific CLI commands. Any platform can be added to the project to build the specific app:

   ```
   $ ionic platform add android
   ```

We will add an Android platform as it will work on all machines, such as Windows, Linux, or Mac. Ionic will download Android-specific default resources such as icons and splash screens, and also add some important plugins by default. A customized keyboard plugin is bundled with the Ionic app.

3. In order to test the app and view it in your browser, use the Ionic `serve` command:

    ```
    $ ionic serve
    ```

    This will open the Ionic app in your default browser.

    The latest Chrome version provides a way to emulate various mobile device screen sizes. Open **Developer Tools** (*F12*), select **Console** from the top-right corner, and select **Emulation**. You can alternatively select the mobile icon from the top-left corner of the window. Please see the following screenshot:

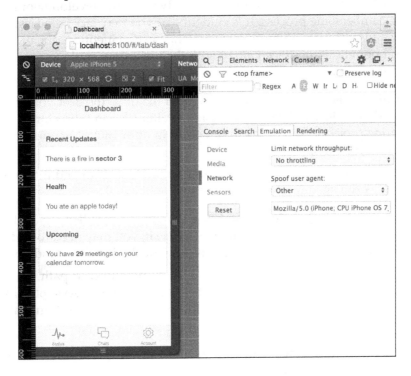

4. Now, we can build the Android App and run it on an actual device or emulator:

```
$ ionic run android
```

This will fire up the emulator if there is no connected device, then start the build process. It will generate the `.apk` file and then deploy it to the emulator or the connected device that is available.

This would be a Eureka moment, seeing your first actual app on the device and playing with it. In the next section we discuss some of the common issues you may have faced during the process and provide solutions for them.

Popular issues faced and solutions

The development environment set up for Ionic Hybrid App development is a lengthy and cumbersome process. It is evident that you may face some issues in installing and setting up all these systems. This section mentions the most common and popular issues faced along with their solutions so that you do not get stuck somewhere:

- **Permission issue [Mac or Linux]**: A lot of the time, the user you are logged in as does not have permission to alter files and directories while creating projects. This problem can occur in npm `install` commands and Ionic `start` commands.

    ◦ **Solution**: Use a `sudo` keyword before any command to run in privileged mode.

- **Unable to find npm global modules**: If you have installed a global npm package using `-g` flag but are unable to use it, you may need to add the npm directory to your path in order to invoke globally installed modules.

    ◦ **Solution**: Add the npm directory location to your path. On Windows, npm can usually be found at `C:\Users\username\AppData\Roaming\npm`. On OS X and Linux it can usually be found at `/usr/local/share/npm`.

- **Git command-line tool not installed**: For Cordova/Ionic plugins to work properly, it fetches code from git repositories.

    ◦ **Solution**: Download and install git from `https://git-scm.com/downloads`.

- **"Failed to run 'android'" or "adb command not found"**: This means that the Android PATH has not been correctly set for this session. Please go to the *Installing Android* section and read how to set the path.
  - ° **Solution**: Set the PATH variable correctly.

If you face any other issues, please research online to find possible solutions for them.

Alternative to installation fuss – Ionic Playground

Ionic Creator Drift Inc. has provided an excellent cloud service called Ionic Playground to build Ionic Apps and fiddle around with Ionic Framework. Ionic Playground is similar to JSFiddle where you can write/edit small Hybrid Apps using Ionic Framework with live preview. It also has the capability to save your app and resume work later using a unique URL. The URL can be shared with multiple people and anyone can fork it to add their own flavor to it. The URL is http://play.ionic.io.

Using Ionic Framework with different Code Editors

Code Editors are an integral part of a development environment and hence it is important to choose the perfect editor that augments the coding style for Ionic. Here we suggest some Code Editors that support Ionic Framework very well.

Brackets

Brackets is a new but promising Code Editor for building JS and HTML5 Apps as it is built using the same technologies. It has the capability to add extensions to augment its features. The Code Editor can be downloaded from http://brackets.io. Brackets has an excellent extension for Ionic, which can be found at http://ionicbrackets.com.

Sublime Text

Sublime Text is the most popular choice among all web developers. It is a very lightweight and fast Code Editor, with full support for JavaScript and HTML5. It also has the capability to add plugins. Ionic also has a plugin for Sublime. Download the Code Editor from `http://sublimetext.com/download`.

Visual Studio

Visual Studio has recently launched support for Ionic by providing starter project templates directly available in the menu itself. You can install them in your Visual Studio after installing Cordova tools. The Ionic Project templates installation can be accessed by going to **Tools | Extension and Updates**, and in the **Online** tab searching for **Ionic**.

Summary

We have learned how to set up the complete development environment for building Hybrid Mobile Apps using Ionic Framework. We have set up the platform environments for iOS and Android. We have also successfully created a dummy app and tested it. In the next chapter we will learn the different templates to bootstrap and the underlying architecture and structure of an Ionic App.

3
Start Building Your First Ionic App

In this chapter, we will build our first Ionic App and build it to test on actual devices. Starting a project seems to be the toughest step but if done well, eases the whole process. It is rightly said, "well begun is half done," so we will learn how to start our project perfectly and create the skeleton for our project. All the options of the starter templates available with Ionic Framework will be explained in detail. In this chapter, we will learn about Ionic Framework while building a sample e-commerce Mobile App. In this chapter, we will discuss the design and architecture for our app. The topics covered in this chapter are as follows:

- Starting a new project:
    - Multiple ways to start a new project

- The anatomy of an Ionic Project:
    - The project's folder structure
    - Main components

- Ionic starter templates:
    - Blank
    - Tabs
    - Side menu
    - Maps

- Design and architecture for an e-commerce sample app – BookStore

In Ionic Framework, starting a project has been made very easy, and using the library is straightforward too. Ionic Framework is perfect for those people who are individual developers looking to launch their Mobile App into the market, or techie entrepreneurs who are planning to start a mobile business. Ionic Framework has a smooth learning curve and reading this book can be used to develop a production-ready Hybrid Mobile App.

All the code samples in the subsequent chapters will be streamlined and organized around building the e-commerce Mobile App talked about in this chapter. In this journey, anyone can learn how to take your ideas from the design phase to market launch.

In this chapter, we will also learn in detail how to test our apps in browsers or emulators. Mobile Apps are very cumbersome to debug as we cannot see the output of console logs from the actual devices or emulators. We will learn about various methods to aid this process and help to resolve multiple issues arising during the development phase.

Starting a new project

Ionic Framework comprises two major parts, one is the library consisting of JavaScript and CSS files, and the other is the CLI tools and cloud services provided for rapid application development. Ionic CLI has already been set up using the installation steps given in the previous chapter. An Ionic App project can be started in multiple ways with or without the installation of the CLI tools and also using a cloud-based service called **Ionic Creator**.

Multiple ways to start a project

There are various methods to start a project as shown in the following sections.

Method 1 – using CDN-hosted library files

An Ionic App majorly requires the Ionic library JS and CSS files for development. These can be referenced directly from the CDN so that our app always uses the latest versions. We do not even require to set up our local environment for this method.

 This method should only be used for developing Mobile Apps using Ionic. To develop Hybrid Mobile Apps you would need to use Ionic CLI.

Ionic library is built on top of the AngularJS framework and hence we need to include its library files too. Ionic library includes two types of JS/CSS files, ones that have AngularJS code bundled to it and the others where the AngularJS code is segregated and needs to be included separately. The link to the Ionic CDN website where the URLs for each of the library files mentioned is `http://code.ionicframework.com/`.

We have to include the JavaScript file and the CSS file in a new `index.html` file, which will be the starting point for our Ionic App. A sample HTML code for the `index.html` would look like the following:

```
<!DOCTYPE html>
<html ng-app="FirstApp">
  <head>
    <title>First Ionic App</title>
    <meta charset="utf-8">
    <meta name="viewport" content="initial-scale=1,
    maximum-scale=1, user-scalable=no, width=device-width">
    <link rel="stylesheet" type="text/css"
    href="http://code.ionicframework.com/1.0.1/css/ionic.min.css">
  </head>
  <body>
    <h1>Bare Minimum App</h1>
    <script type="text/javascript"
    src="http://code.ionicframework.com/1.0.1/js/
    ionic.bundle.min.js"></script>
    <script type="text/javascript">
      angular.module("FirstApp", ['ionic'])
      .config(function(){
      })
      .run(function($ionicPlatform){
      });
    </script>
  </body>
</html>
```

The preceding code is just for starting your app. You need to organize your app-specific JS and CSS code into separate files accordingly as we proceed. Also, in order to view mobile-specific content you can add some Ionic specific directives or code to the preceding HTML file to test the correct output. Please replace the `h1` tag in the file with the following code:

```
<ion-pane>
  <ion-header-bar class="bar-stable">
    <h1 class="title">Ionic Blank Starter</h1>
```

```
      </ion-header-bar>
      <ion-content>
      </ion-content>
    </ion-pane>
```

Method 2 – using Ionic Creator to design a prototype and start a project

Ionic Creator is a drag and drop-based cloud console to design and prototype Ionic Apps. Ionic Creator provides an easy-to-use interface to create views and interactions for your Ionic App. We can link multiple views to create complete use cases and flow. It is the easiest way to start a new project and build your app rapidly. It also contains practically all the Ionic components that can be customized from the UI options themselves as shown in the following screenshot:

After designing your app using Ionic Creator, you can export it to code it further and include complex functionality. The code can be exported in the following ways:

- **Ionic CLI**: Two commands mentioned in the UI with a unique project ID to download.
- **ZIP File**: Downloading the zip file directly using this option.
- **Raw HTML**: An integrated HTML code is generated, which can be copied and pasted. The following screenshot shows the popup view to export and download your Ionic Creator project:

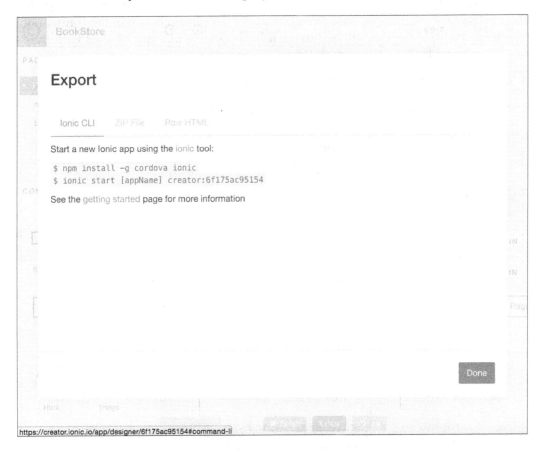

This method is mostly suitable for people who have beginner-level knowledge of HTML and CSS. They can start their project using downloaded content from the Ionic Creator project. The previous screenshot shows exporting the content.

Projects being developed without setting up the local environment and CLI can use a cloud-based service by Adobe called Phonegap Build to build apps. This service can generate iOS, Android, and Windows builds without installing the development environments locally. Ionic also recently launched a new tool called **Ionic Lab**, which can be used for this. We will discuss this further in the last chapter.

Method 3 – using Ionic CLI locally

Ionic CLI can be used to start a new project using the command used in the previous chapter. Ionic CLI's `start` command creates a new project with a complete folder structure and sample code from one of the templates chosen in the command. There are multiple flags mentioned in the following table that can be used with the `start` command:

```
$ ionic start [OPTIONS] <PATH> [template]
```

Options can be set using the flags in the following table:

Flag	Description

`[--appname	-a]`	Name for your app that is easily readable (use quotes). Example:
		`ionic start -appname "MyApp" myapp blank`
		Or:
		`ionic start -a "MyApp" myapp blank`

`[--id	-i]`	Unique package name set for the app that will be set in the config as `<widget_id>`:
		`ionic start -id com.myorg.myapp myapp blank`
		Or:
		`ionic start -i com.myorg.myapp myapp blank`

`[--no-cordova	-w]`	Use this flag if you do not want to create a Cordova project:
		`ionic start --no-cordova myapp blank`
		Or:
		`ionic start --w myapp blank`

`[--sass	-s]`	Set up the project to use Sass CSS precompiling:
		`ionic start --sass myapp blank`
		Or:
		`ionic start --s myapp blank`

`[--list	-l]`	List the starter templates available: `ionic start --list`

In the next section, we will learn about the different sections and components of the app generated during the start phase of the app using any template.

The anatomy of Ionic Project

Ionic Project is referred to in the project setup using the Ionic CLI tools locally. The later section will describe the main components of Ionic App that are relevant for the projects started using CDN files or Ionic Creator. In order to understand Ionic Project, we need to understand the project structure and the sections in the Ionic App code.

Project folder structure and important files

The Ionic App project folder structure includes folders for Cordova files, native platform code, and web content code. It also contains configuration files for dependency managers used in an Ionic App as shown in the following screenshot:

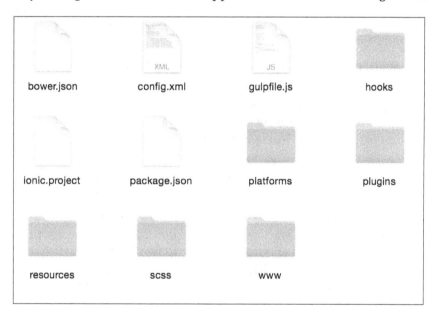

We will discuss briefly the important folders and files along with their purpose. These important folders and files are:

- `bower.json` (file): This is used as a configuration file for Bower, dependency managers for frontend libraries, and frameworks. The library directory for storage is written in a separate file `.bowerrc` and is set to `www/lib` by default.

- `config.xml` (file): This file contains the configuration settings for the Cordova project. It is used to define meta information about the app and permissions required for the apps to be installed on specific platforms. It also includes the Cordova plugins used in the app. To read more about the different sections and tags available to be put in `config.xml` see `https://cordova.apache.org/docs/en/4.0.0/config_ref_index.md.html`.

- `gulpfile.js` (file): This is used as config script for Gulp, the build management system used for Ionic web content. It has multiple plugins used for different tasks such as concatenation, auto-installing Bower, and compiling Sass files to CSS files.

- `ionic.project` (file): This file is used to store meta information regarding Ionic Project and associated Ionic.io cloud account services associated with it.

- `package.json` (file): Most of the systems such as Gulp and Bower are installed and managed using Node's package manage NPM, and `package.json` is the file to store versions of the NPM packages installed in Ionic Project.

- `hooks` (folder): This folder contains code for Cordova hooks, which is a way to execute some code during a life cycle event in a Cordova build life cycle. Ionic utilizes the `after_prepare` hook to inject platform-specific CSS and HTML code.

- `platforms` (folder): This folder consists of the platform subfolders that are added to Ionic Project. The subfolders contain native projects for the Ionic App.

- `plugins` (folder): The `plugins` folder contains Cordova plugin subfolders, which include the JS library and native codebase for the specific plugins. The plugins are added and managed using the CLI commands, which we will learn about in future chapters. Cordova plugins can be developed by any developer and can be integrated using a `git url/repo`.

- `resources` (folder): A Mobile App requires static resources such as icons and splash screens. Each platform has specialized requirements regarding the sizes and format for icons. Ionic CLI provides special commands to automatically generate platform-specific resources from generic ones.

- scss (folder): scss consists of .scss files based on the SASS framework. SASS is an extension of CSS3, which empowers the developer with multiple constructs to organize CSS code of the Ionic App. It includes features such as nested rules, variables, mixins, and more. The default file ionic.app.scss contains important base variables such as theme colors and font paths. SASS is not necessary for developing Ionic Apps but if you know the technology, you can add your scss files to this folder and Gulp will automatically compile them into CSS.

- www (folder): This is the most important folder that contains the actual code for Ionic App. It contains the HTML, CSS, JavaScript, and other static files such as images, fonts, and so on. Ionic Project, by default, creates subfolders under this folder for css, img, js, and templates (HTML) code.

It is recommended to organize your code into different folders, one for each feature, and include all other necessary files such as controllers, directives, and services in the same folder.

Main components

The main code lies inside the www folder. The Ionic App at its base is an AngularJS app with an Ionic module injected and multiple directives being used. We will discuss the main constructs and components in a basic Ionic App, which are the most essential.

The index.html file

The most important file and the starting point of your Ionic App is index.html. It should contain important meta tags for the viewport to be able to resize properly on mobile devices. If you have created an Ionic Project using CLI, then you do not need to worry about it. If you are trying to create an Ionic App manually, please include this meta tag in the head section of your index.html:

```
<meta name="viewport" content="initial-scale=1, maximum-scale=1,
user-scalable=no, width=device-width">
```

Also, please check the references to the Ionic bundle script or AngularJS script if the bundled library is not used. Also, please check that cordova.js is injected as this reference will be required only after Cordova builds the app, and will give a 404 error during the development phase and testing on browsers:

```
<!-- ionic/angularjs js -->
<script src="lib/ionic/js/ionic.bundle.js"></script>
<!-- cordova script (this will be a 404 during development) -->
<script src="cordova.js"></script>
```

The next important thing is the `ng-app` directive and the value given to the attribute. The `ng-app` directive should be present as an attribute on either body tag or the root HTML tag. This is required to bootstrap the Angular app using the same name in `app.js` while defining the root angular module. The body tag can include any Ionic components. We will discuss some common important Ionic directives that will form the base for an Ionic App.

App.js and the root module

The next important file is the `app.js`, which will be used to bootstrap the Ionic/Angular app. The name of the module should match the value given to the `ng-app` attribute in `index.html`.

It is also required to inject the `ionic` module dependency into our root module so that we can use Ionic library directives and other constructs. We can inject any other modules into the root module, for example, the services, controllers, or custom directives that we write for our app.

In a Hybrid Mobile App, we have to call native functionalities using the Cordova plugin. It is compulsory to listen to Cordova's device `ready` event, which lets us know that the native Cordova library has been loaded and our HTML code can call native functionality. Similarly, in Ionic, there is a facility to register a callback in the `$ionicPlatform.ready` event, which fires after the Cordova's device `ready` event. We should check the status of native plugins or call any native functionality inside this `ready` event callback. The default code in the `run` block of the root module when you create an Ionic App is as follows:

```
angular.module('starter', ['ionic']) // starter.services etc can be
added
.run(function($ionicPlatform) {
  $ionicPlatform.ready(function() {
    // Hide the accessory bar by default (remove this to show the
    accessory bar above the keyboard
    // for form inputs)
    if (window.cordova && window.cordova.plugins &&
    window.cordova.plugins.Keyboard) {
      cordova.plugins.Keyboard.hideKeyboardAccessoryBar(true);
      cordova.plugins.Keyboard.disableScroll(true);
    }
    if (window.StatusBar) {
      // org.apache.cordova.statusbar required
      StatusBar.styleLightContent();
    }
  });
})
```

Inside the `ready` function we are detecting whether the keyboard plugin is present in our Ionic App, and we are hiding the keyboard accessory bar and disabling the scroll. You can change these values as per your requirements in your app.

Simple content directives – ion-content and ion-pane

In a basic Ionic App, the two important directives used to put content in are `<ion-content>` and `<ion-pane>`. Generally, the content is put in a navigation view, but navigation directives will be discussed in the next chapter. In order to create very basic apps, direct content directives can be used in the main file or by using templates for different routes.

ion-content

The `ion-content` directive is used to wrap the content of a view, which can also be configured to use Ionic's custom scroll view, or the built-in scrolling of the web view. It is important to note that this directive gets its own child scope and thus any models inside this directive should be referenced accordingly. Some important attributes that can be used along with this directive are given in the following table:

Attribute [type]	Details
direction [string]	Specifying the direction to scroll. x, y, or xy. Default is y.
scroll [boolean]	It specifies whether to allow scrolling of content. Default is true.
overflow-scroll [boolean]	It specifies whether to use overflow scrolling instead of Ionic scroll. The `$ionicConfigProvider` object can be used in `config` block to set this default.
start-x [string]	Initial horizontal scroll position. Default to 0.
start-y [string]	Initial vertical scroll position. Default to 0.
has-bouncing [boolean]	It specifies whether to allow scrolling to bounce past the boundaries of content. Defaults to true on iOS and false on Android.

ion-pane

The `ion-pane` directive is a simple container for adding content. It just adds a class `pane` to the element in which the contents are encapsulated.

The following is the usage of this directive:

```
<ion-pane>
...
</ion-pane>
```

The Ionic starter template

In the Ionic CLI, you can start a new project using a specific template. There are predefined templates available in the Ionic CLI toolset. They all provide a starting point for developers and also act as a skeleton for your new app. We have already seen the command to start a new project with a specific template earlier on in this chapter. If we want to choose the `tabs` template, then the command would look like the following:

```
$ ionic start TabsDemo tabs
```

We will be discussing the important files in each of the templates.

The blank template

It contains the bare minimum code for an Ionic App. It injects Ionic and Angular dependencies into your `index.html` and creates separate folders for CSS, `js`, and `img`. It also provides a basic view code in the body tag of `index.html` to show `ion-pane` and `ion-header` content.

The tabs template

The `tabs` template provides an app layout with the bottom three tabs and multiple views for each tab. It sets up the controllers and templates for different states. In Ionic, the open source and popular router called UI-Router is used for creating states/routes. We will learn about it in detail in the next chapter.

In the `app.js config` block, the states are defined using the `$stateProvider` object. In this template, an abstract state is created for the tabs as it will be shown for all views and then the states for subsequent views are created.

In `index.html`, the `<ion-nav-bar>` directive is used to display a top navbar on all the views. It also contains the `<ion-nav-view>` directive that will act as a placeholder for all the default layout/templates associated with the abstract state for showing the tabs on all views of the app:

```
<ion-nav-bar class="bar-stable">
  <ion-nav-back-button>
  </ion-nav-back-button>
</ion-nav-bar>
<ion-nav-view></ion-nav-view>
```

All the template files are present in the `templates` folder inside the www folder. The `tabs.html` file is associated with the main tabs state and uses the `<ion-tabs>` directive, which consists of one or more `<ion-tab>` directives to represent each tab. We can set specific properties of the directive such as `icon-on` and `icon-off` to show an active icon and non-active icon respectively. We also create named `<ion-nav-view>` directives under each tab directive to create containers for showing templates for different tabs:

```
<ion-tabs class="tabs-icon-top tabs-color-active-positive">
  <!-- Dashboard Tab -->
  <ion-tab title="Status" icon-off="ion-ios-pulse"
  icon-on="ion-ios-pulse-strong" href="#/tab/dash">
    <ion-nav-view name="tab-dash"></ion-nav-view>
  </ion-tab>
  <!-- Chats Tab -->
  <ion-tab title="Chats" icon-off="ion-ios-chatboxes-outline"
  icon-on="ion-ios-chatboxes" href="#/tab/chats">
    <ion-nav-view name="tab-chats"></ion-nav-view>
  </ion-tab>
  <!-- Account Tab -->
  <ion-tab title="Account" icon-off="ion-ios-gear-outline"
  icon-on="ion-ios-gear" href="#/tab/account">
    <ion-nav-view name="tab-account"></ion-nav-view>
  </ion-tab>
</ion-tabs>
```

The `templates` folder also has a separate file for each tab view named `tab-<view_name>.html`. The code in each file consists of one `<ion-view>` directive on the top with the `view-title` attribute to set the header bar for our app. It also consists of an `<ion-content>` directive to contain the actual content of that particular view.

The controllers for each of the views are bound in the `app.js` in the respective state representing the tab view for account, chats, and dashboard.

The sidemenu template

The sidemenu template contains a layout where a side menu drawer is used for primary navigation. Ionic Project can be created with this template by mentioning the name of this template in the Ionic start command as follows:

```
$ ionic start MenuDemo sidemenu
```

This template has only the <ion-nav-view> directive in the body tag of index. html. The main state that is marked as abstract in app.js will load the template templates/menu.html and associate the controller AppCtrl with it. According to the other states defined in app.js, respective templates will be loaded into the menucontent ion-view directive present in menu.html. The code for menu.html should be as follows:

```html
<ion-side-menus enable-menu-with-back-views="false">
  <ion-side-menu-content>
    <ion-nav-bar class="bar-stable">
      <ion-nav-back-button>
      </ion-nav-back-button>
      <ion-nav-buttons side="left">
        <button class="button button-icon button-clear
        ion-navicon" menu-toggle="left">
        </button>
      </ion-nav-buttons>
    </ion-nav-bar>
    <ion-nav-view name="menuContent"></ion-nav-view>
  </ion-side-menu-content>
  <ion-side-menu side="left">
    <ion-header-bar class="bar-stable">
      <h1 class="title">Left</h1>
    </ion-header-bar>
    <ion-content>
      <ion-list>
        <ion-item menu-close ng-click="login()">
          Login
        </ion-item>
        <ion-item menu-close href="#/app/search">
          Search
        </ion-item>
        <ion-item menu-close href="#/app/browse">
          Browse
        </ion-item>
```

```
        <ion-item menu-close href="#/app/playlists">
          Playlists
        </ion-item>
      </ion-list>
    </ion-content>
  </ion-side-menu>
</ion-side-menus>
```

The `ion-content` directive in this file contains an `<ion-side-menu-content>` directive, which contains the view displayed in the center or the main view. It contains another subview `<ion-nav-view name="menucontent">`, which will show respective templates for each state representing the menu item views. The links to the views are contained in the `<ion-content>` directive under `<ion-list>`.

The maps template

The `maps` template contains a layout where a map is loaded on the main view itself. It includes the controller for the view and a directive for showing the map on Ionic App. It has a feature of showing the current position on the map. In order to create a project using this template, please use the following command:

$ ionic start MapsDemo maps

The `index.html` file contains an `<ion-header>` directive, an `<ion-content>` directive containing the custom `<map>` directive, and the `<ion-footer>` directive. It is important to load the Google Maps API script to display the map. The controller is associated on the `body` tag using the `ng-controller` directive attribute:

```
<body ng-app="starter" ng-controller="MapCtrl">
  <ion-header-bar class="bar-stable">
    <h1 class="title">Map</h1>
  </ion-header-bar>
  <ion-content scroll="false">
    <map on-create="mapCreated(map)"></map>
  </ion-content>
  <ion-footer-bar class="bar-stable">
    <a ng-click="centerOnMe()" class="button button-icon icon
    ion-navigate"></a>
  </ion-footer-bar>

  <script src="https://maps.googleapis.com/maps/api/js?
  key=AIzaSyB16sGmIekuGIvYOfNoW9T44377IU2d2Es&sensor=true">
  </script>
</body>
```

E-commerce sample app – BookStore

From the subsequent sections, we will be creating a sample app while learning about different Ionic components and features. Using this approach, you will be able to develop a complete app at the end of this chapter. The code samples used in the following chapters will be available online.

E-commerce is a hot category for Mobile Apps these days, so we will be creating an e-commerce app for books and will call it BookStore. The features of this app and its basic architecture is discussed here.

Features

The e-commerce sample app BookStore will be a basic shopping and book management app that has a list of books with the ability to buy or rent them. The proposed features we intend to cover in the code samples are as follows:

- List of book categories
- Book listings under categories and popular/featured listings
- User account section:
  - Login/register
  - Profile
  - Purchased books/rented books
  - Maps
- Shopping section:
  - Add to cart
  - Edit cart
  - Checkout

Architecture and design

We will be using the side menu template as a skeleton for this app. The side menu will contain links for the user account section and the categories list. We will be using a dummy REST API to source data for the mobile application. The Ionic App will contain a basic service layer consisting of multiple Angular services to integrate with this service.

Summary

We learned to start building an Ionic App using multiple options and different skeleton templates. The chapter also included information about important Ionic directives used for basic content in the Mobile App. We have also discussed the sample app we will be developing during the next chapters.

4
Navigation and Routing in an Ionic App

In any Mobile App, navigation and routing plays the most important part. It defines the backbone of the mobile experience and provides ease of access if implemented perfectly. In this chapter, we will discuss the various options available in Ionic Framework to define routing in an application. Ionic Framework has included an open source routing module called **UI Router**, which was developed along with the Angular UI bootstrap library. UI Router is a preferred routing module over the in-built Angular ngRoute module. The following important topics will be discussed in this chapter:

- Introduction to Angular UI Router:
    - States and URLs
    - Nested states and views
    - Multiple and named views
    - State parameters
    - State events and resolve

- Ionic header and footer
- Ionic tabs
- Ionic side menus
- Navigation and back menu
- Navigation and layout to be used in BookStore

Introduction to Angular UI Router

The core of Ionic Framework is an open source routing module called Angular UI Router. It implements states that are a part of a state machine represented by the complete app. In a normal Angular app, we use ngRoute, which defines different routes, each of which can be associated with only a single ng-view and one corresponding templateUrl. In the UI Router, routes are represented by states (discussed in the following chapter).

States and URLs

In an app using the UI Router, the views are not tied up to the URL and hence you can change the parts of the app even without changing the URL. In any mobile app, the views are not so simple that they can be changed wholly but there is a complex hierarchy of views and sub-views that change based on different states. Due to this reason it is better to maintain states instead of routes and hence Ionic chose to use the Angular UI Router instead of ngRoute. States are also defined in the config section of an angular module.

We will learn how to create a state by adding a simple view for our sample app. A new state is created with the name homeView, which will be the default view shown after the app is bootstrapped. It will be associated with a controller and a template string or template URL similar to the route:

```
angular.module('BookStore', ['ionic'])
.config(['$stateProvider','$urlRouterProvider',
  function mainAppConfig($stateProvider,$urlRouterProvider){
    $urlRouterProvider.otherwise('/home')
    $stateProvider.state('homeView', {
      url: '/home',
      template: '<p>App Home View!</p>',
  .   controller: 'HomeController'
    });
  }]
)
```

The state that we have created will be accessible using the URL http://<domain-name>/home and will be opened by default because of the code $urlRouterProvider.otherwise('/home').

We can associate a template like the previous one or give a URL to the `html` template using the `templateUrl` property on the state. Whenever this state is loaded, the template HTML code will be injected into the `<ion-nav-view>` directive of the parent state. In this case, for the root state, we should be adding the `<ion-nav-view>` directive to the `index.html` file with some initial content:

```
<ion-nav-view>
  Loading View...
</ion-nav-view>
```

The perfect way to decide whether a state should exist or not is by ensuring that a state adheres to the following principles:

- A state represents a section of your app that is navigable from one or multiple other states and displays important information about your app

- A state encapsulates important markup and logic in terms of a template and a controller

- Sometimes, multiple states would have some part of the view common and the best approach to implement such a requirement is to create separate states and use state hierarchy to model the commonalities

Nested states and views

We have already seen how to create a simple state, but we would hardly have an app with simple states. In order to represent a complex view, we would divide our state into some sub states representing sub sections of the views.

We can create nested states in the following multiple ways.

Using the dot notation

In order to create a nested state, we can use `.` to write the name of the child state after the parent state. If the parent state is named as `homeView`, we can register a nested state `menu` by naming it `.state ('homeView.menu', {})`. The Angular UI Router module by default sets the state before the dot operator as the parent of the state object.

Using the parent property

Nested states can also be created by using a `parent` property on the state object passed as a second argument to the `state` method of `$stateProvider`. The name of the parent state can be set as a string value to the `parent` property:

```
$stateProvider.state('menu',{
  parent: 'homeView',
  templateUrl:'homeView.menu.html',
  controller: 'MenuController'
}
```

Using object-based states

We can use objects instead of strings to set the `parent` property of the state object:

```
var homeView = { name:'homeView', ... };
var menu = { name: 'homeView.menu',
             parent: homeView,
             templateUrl:'homeView.menu.html'
           }
```

States can be registered in any order and a child state can be registered before the parent state. It will queue the child state registration until the parent is registered.

No two state names can be the same. With the dot notation or without dot notation, the names of the states need to be different even if the two states have different parents.

Views for nested views

If the application is in a particular state, and the state is active, then all its ancestor states are active by default. The child states will load their templates into their parents' `<ion-nav-view>` directives.

Ways to transition to a state

In order to transition to a specific state or make any state active, there are multiple ways available.

You can use an anchor tag and set the `href` attribute to # followed by the URL for the state. For example, if the URL is set to `/home/main`, then the `href` attribute value should be `#/home/main`:

```
<a href="#/home/main"> Main Link </a>
```

Another way to link states in HTML is to use the `ui-sref` directive, which allows the developer to pass in the state name instead of state URL:

```
<a ui-sref="homeView.main"> Main Link </a>
```

If we want to transition to a particular state from JavaScript, then we can use a method on the `$state` object that can be injected into any controller. Please note that in `ui.sref` you give the value starting from the parent template. For example, if you are giving a link in `index.html` then you should give `ui-sref='homeView.main'` but if the link is in `homeView.html` then give `ui-sref='main'`:

```
<a ui-sref="homeView.main"> Main Link </a>
```

We will be working with a new Ionic Project using a `blank` starter project template and use the code snippets given along with the chapters to build the BookStore e-commerce sample app.

Abstract state

In the UI router, there is a provision to define an abstract state, which can have child states but it cannot be activated itself. This state cannot be transitioned to and it is activated automatically when one of its descendants is activated. The use cases for using an abstract state is when we want to use a state for layouts only, when a URL needs to be appended to all states, and to provide common data or resolved dependencies to all child states.

Abstract states would still require a `<ion-nav-view/>` directive in the template:

```
.state('homeView',{
  abstract: true,
  url: '/home',
  templateUrl: 'homeView.html'
});
```

Multiple and named views

In a complex mobile app, we would want multiple sections of our app to change according to different states. In Ionic also, we can have more than one `<ion-nav-view/>` in a single template by giving them a named attribute. We can have only one maximum unnamed `ion-nav-view` in a template.

When setting multiple views in a state, we have to use the `views` property, which will contain the name of the views as keys and objects for each view (`templateUrl`, `controller`, and so on) as values.

Abstract states would still require a `<ion-nav-view/>` directive in the template:

```
$stateProvider
.state('homeView.books', {
  abstract:true,
  url:'/books',
  templateUrl: 'homeView.books.html'
})
.state('homeView.books.list',{
  views: {
    filters: {
      templateUrl:'homeView.books.filters.html'
    },
    list: {
      templateUrl:'homeView.books.list.html'
    }
  }
});
```

In a state where the `views` property is set, it automatically ignores the template, `templateUrl` or `templateProvider`, so if you want to set a template, then you need to define an abstract state as a parent defining the layout. Also, remember that in Ionic, by default `<ion-nav-view/>` has such CSS styling that it takes the whole screen size and the last named view will always be on top. You have to write custom CSS styling to achieve your design.

View names – relative versus abstract

In the previous example, by default the named view is expected on the parent state. If we want to reference a specific named view of any ascendant state, then we can use @ to write the exact view like `<view-name>@<state-name>`.

State parameters

URL routing is very important along with the state mechanics defined for the app. Using the power of URL routing we can send data or parameters in the URL itself, which helps in identifying the state along with some unique identifiers for the state. There are various types of parameter that can be passed to a route or state.

Basic parameters

The URL can have dynamic parts, which can contain any value, and the controller should be able to access the value passed. You can use a : character or { } to define a dynamic URL part, which is called a basic parameter:

```
$stateProvider
.state('homeView.books.detail', {
  url: "/books/:bookId",
  templateUrl: 'books.detail.html',
  controller: function ($stateParams) {
    // If we got here from a url of /contacts/42
    expect($stateParams).toBe({bookId: "42"});
    // expect() is a method of Jasmine Framework Unit Testing
    Code
  }
})
```

Alternatively, the basic parameter can also be defined using curly braces:

```
url: "/books/{bookId}"
```

Regex parameters

We can restrict the values passed in the url parameters by using a regular expression inside curly brackets in the url value of the state. For example:

```
url: "/books/{bookId:[0-9]{1,8}}"
```

The previous line specifies that the bookId parameter can be digits only and its length can vary from 1 to 8.

Query parameters

Query parameters are similar to the HTML query string parameters commonly used. You can send parameters in the URL itself after the ? symbol as key value pairs.

Single parameter

Sample URL structure to represent single query parameter is as follows:

```
url: "/books?bookId" // will match to url of /books?bookId=value
```

Multiple parameters

Sample URL structure to represent multiple query parameters is as follows:

```
url: "/books?bookId&category" // will match to
/books?bookId=v1&category=c1
```

The $stateParams service

This is an in-built service in the UI Router module, which provides access to each state parameter in the controller. It is important to note that parameters only specific to that state and not its ascendants will be available in the controller. An example of URLs and corresponding $stateParams object is as follows; in this example it is mentioned how the bookId parameter can be accessed using $stateParams:

```
// If url is of type 'books/:bookId/details?section'
// Actual Url hit is   /books/23/details?section=4
console.log($stateParams);
// Console Output:
{ bookId: 23, section: 4}
```

State events and resolve

Important angular events are fired during the management of states in an app. Whenever the state changes from one state to another, there are a handful of events that are broadcasted from the $rootScope and are available for all the controller scopes to listen. If we want to handle them globally, we can use the $on method on the $rootScope variable to handle them. The code would look like this:

```
$rootScope.$on('<event-name>',function handler(eventArgs ...){});
```

The lists of events available are as follows:

Event	Description
$stateChangeStart	This event is fired when state transition begins: ```$rootScope.$on('$stateChangeStart',` `function(event, toState, toParams,` `fromState,` `fromParams){ ... });```
$stateNotFound	The event is fired when the state requested for is not found in that app. The event is broadcasted allowing any handlers a single chance to deal with the error.
$stateChangeSuccess	This event is fired when the state change is successful, for example, the transition from one state to another has ended.

Event	Description
`$stateChangeError`	This event occurs if there is some error while transitioning from one state to another. This event also occurs if any error is found in the resolve functions. One must listen to this error to catch all errors.

Resolve

Each and every state can have a property `resolve`, which is helpful to provide content or data to the controller. `resolve` is an optional map of dependencies that should be injected to the controller.

A useful feature of `resolve` is that it can also contain promises, which can help us to get data using AJAX requests. Also, the controller is not initialized for a state before all the resolve dependencies. The `resolve` object contains key and value pairs. The key can be any string whereas the value can be a function or a string. If the value of `resolve` is a string, it represents a service in the same module, and if it is a function, it should return a value or any promise.

The code for an example `resolve` block in a state definition looks like this:

```
$stateProvider.state('homeView',{
  url:'/home',
  resolve: {
    information: function(infoService) {
      return infoService.getInfo();
    },
    about: 'aboutService'
  }
});
```

Ionic header and footer

Ionic has many directives to help common layouts in mobile apps. Ionic headers and footers are important directives for showing proper context for any view in a mobile app. The exact directives, name and their usage are detailed as follows.

The <ion-header-bar> directive

This directive adds a fixed header bar above any content. You can also add a subheader by adding a CSS class `bar-subheader` on the second `<ion-header-bar>` directive, which will be shown below the primary header. The sample code for usage is as follows:

```
<ion-header-bar align-title="left" class="bar-positive">
  <div class="buttons">
    <button class="button" ng-click="back()">Back</button>
  </div>
  <h1 class="title">All about Books</h1>
  <div class="buttons"> <button class="button">Logout</button>
  </div>
</ion-header-bar>
```

There are two attributes available on the directive to add functionality to the header bar as shown in the following table:

Attribute	Type	Details
align-title (optional)	string	This property tells how to align the title. By default it will align as per the platform, for example, left in Android and center in iOS. Available: `left`, `right`, or `center`
no-tap-scroll (optional)	boolean	It will control the property of taping the header to scroll the view to the top. If set to `true`, the view will be scrolled and the opposite if set to `false`. It defaults to `false`. Available: `true` or `false`

The <ion-footer-bar> directive

This directive adds a fixed footer bar below some content similar to the header bar. There can be a subfooter by adding the class `bar-subfooter`. The sample code for usage is as follows:

```
<ion-footer-bar align-title="left" class="bar-assertive">
  <div class="buttons">
    <button class="button">Back</button>
  </div>
  <h1 class="title">All about Books</h1>
  <div class="buttons" ng-click="logout()">
    <button class="button">Logout</button>
  </div>
</ion-footer-bar>
```

There is only one attribute available on the directive to add functionality to the footer bar as shown in the following table:

Attribute	Type	Details
align-title (optional)	string	This property tells how to align the title on the footer. Available: left, right, or center

Ionic Tabs

Ionic Tabs is a collection of important directives for creating a tab-based layout for a section of your mobile app. We have already seen how the tabs directive is used in the tabs starter template.

Ionic Tabs is a collection of two directives and one service. The directives are <ion-tabs> used to define the collection or group of tabs, and the <ion-tab>, directive, which is used to define a specific tab. The service $ionicTabsDelegate is used to control the tabs from JavaScript in order to select a specific tab.

The <ion-tabs> directive

It provides a multi-tabbed interface with a set of tabs and multiple views that can be switched. The tabs CSS classes are used to set the styling of the tabs group. The class name tabs should be used along with the following classes for specific styles:

CSS class	Description
tabs-<theme_name>	Defines the color of the tabs, for example, tabs-positive, tabs-calm, and so on.
tabs-icon-only	It will show tabs with icons only. You have to include the icon in the tab directive.
tabs-icon-top	This class puts the icon at the top and text at the bottom.
tabs-icon-left	This class puts the icon on the left.

The `<ion-tabs>` directive has one attribute that enables you to pass a custom handle for the delegate as shown in the following table:

Attribute	Type	Details
delegate-handle (optional)	string	The handle used to identify these tabs with `$ionicTabsDelegate`.

The <ion-tab> directive

Inside the `<ion-tab>` directive, we can use one or multiple `<ion-tab>` directives. The tab content can be included in the `<ion-tab>` directive, which will be shown only when the specific tab is selected. Each `<ion-tab>` has its own navigation history and should include its own named `<ion-nav-view>`.

The following is the usage of this directive:

```
<ion-tab
   title="Custom Tab"
   icon="ion-star"
   href="#/book/favourites"
   on-select="goToFavourites()"
   on-deselect="unsetFavourites()">
</ion-tab>
```

The important attributes available on the `<ion-tab>` directive and their functions is outlined in the following table:

Attribute	Type	Details
title	string	The title of the tab view
href (optional)	string	The link that will be opened if the tab is tapped
icon (optional)	string	The icon of the tab, which if set, is default for `icon-on` and `icon-off`
icon-off (optional)	string	The icon of the tab when it is not active
icon-on (optional)	string	The icon of the tab when it is active
badge (optional)	expression	A number or small character shown on the icon tab
on-select (optional)	string	This method will be called when tab is selected

Attribute	Type	Details
on-deselect (optional)	string	This method will be called when tab is deselected

Ionic side menu

Ionic side menus also consist of multiple directives that help in achieving a layout with one or many side menus. It defines the layout of a section of your app. All the directives for this purpose are defined in this section.

The <ion-side-menus> directive

It is container for the ionSideMenu directive and the main content. A left-side menu, right-side menu, or both can be added to the layout of your app. This directive/ element must have at least two children, one should be an <ion-side-menu-content> directive, which will load the views of the app, and one or more <ion-side-menu>.

The different attributes available to be used with this directive are as follows:

Attribute	Type	Details
enable-menu-with-back-views (optional)	bool	This attribute determines whether the side menu is enabled when the back button is showing. If it is set to true then the menu-toggle elements will be shown, and if the value is false, they will be hidden.
delegate-handle (optional)	string	The handle used to pass the delegate to manage side menus.

The <ion-side-menu> directive

This directive is the place for side menu content. The side menu list view and other content can be included in this directive.

The following is the usage of this directive:

```
<ion-side-menu
  side="left"
  width="200"
  is-enabled="shouldLeftSideMenuBeEnabled()">
</ion-side-menu>
```

This directive has only three attributes: `side` for defining the side it will slide from, `width` to set the width of the side menu container, and `is-enabled` to set an expression/function to evaluate whether the specific side menu should be enabled or not.

The <ion-side-menu-content> directive

This is the container for the main visible content. It can contain `<ion-nav-view>` to show different views based on the state changes. It is always a sibling to the `ionSideMenu` directive.

The following is the usage of this directive:

```
<ion-side-menu-content
    edge-drag-threshold="true"
    drag-content="true">
</ion-side-menu-content>
```

This directive has two attributes — `edge-drag-threshold`, which defines whether content drag can be enabled or start below a threshold distance from the edge, and `drag-content`, which enables whether content inside this directive can be dragged or not.

Other important directives

In order to work with side menus there are some more directives to be used:

- `menu-close` is an attribute directive that closes a currently opened side menu. This can be used on a link to navigate to a new view, which would close the side menu. It also resets the view's navigation history and removes the back button.

- `menu-toggle` is an attribute that can be set on a button or icon used to toggle a side menu. The specific side menu such as `left` or `right`, can be set to this attribute value.

- `expose-aside-when` is an attribute that controls when the side menu should be kept open. In the case of large tablets, the side menu will always be opened. This directive should be given in the `ionSideMenu` directive.

Navigation and back menus

Ionic Framework has strong navigation support in the form of various directives such as `ionNavView`, `ionView`, `ionNavBar`, and so on. Ionic stores and maintains the navigation history in the mobile app. It dictates the transitions appropriately. An app section can have multiple views, which maintain separate navigation histories.

The UI Router module and states are an integral part of the design for the navigation concepts. The `<ion-nav-view>` directive has already been explained in the first section while defining the UI Router module.

`<ion-view>` is another directive that should be used as a container for the content of any view. It should have a `<ion-content>` directive and can have header and navbar information. It defines the title of the parent `ionNavBar` using the `view-title` attribute. There are other attributes such as `cache-view` to enable caching, `hide-back-button` to define whether the back button should be displayed or not, and `hide-nav-bar` attribute to define whether to hide the parent `ionNavBar` or not:

- `<ion-nav-bar>` is another directive that is created along with the `<ion-nav-view>` directive and shows a top bar that will be modified as soon as the state changes. We can add a back button to be shown using a `<ion-nav-back-button>` directive. We can also add some custom buttons using the `<ion-nav-buttons>` directive.

- `<ion-nav-title>` is a directive that can be used inside the `<ion-nav-view>` directive to override the title set in the navbar with any custom title or HTML content as a title.

Navigation and layout to be used in BookStore

In our sample app, BookStore, we will use a side menu layout throughout. The side menu will contain the links to different sections such as account, orders, checkout, and categories.

The top categories will also be directly accessible from the side menu. The side menu content will show the main views. All the views will have navbar buttons to show **Logout** and **User Account** icon buttons for swift navigation.

Summary

We have learned all about different ways to implement navigation and routing in a Hybrid Mobile Application. We have also learned how to define navigation and view hierarchy for complex views and Mobile Apps. We have also learned about all the available directives and options to use different functionalities to define views and navigation in a Mobile App. In the next chapter, we will come to know about different available components that can be used in our sample e-commerce app.

5
Accessorizing Your App with Ionic Components

We have learnt to build the skeleton and base for a Mobile App. An actual app would contain multiple use cases and complex views, which would include many more elements and components. Ionic Framework equips developers with a multitude of reusable components and directives that they can use to develop apps rapidly. There are two categories of reusable components: CSS components for styling elements, and JS components for logic and interactions. The topics we will be discussing in this chapter are:

- Ionic CSS components
  - Header and footer
  - Buttons
  - Lists
  - Cards
  - Forms
  - Input elements
  - Tabs
  - Grid
  - Utility styles

- Ionic JS components
  - Actionsheet
  - Backdrop
  - Form inputs

- ° Gestures and events
- ° Lists
- ° Loading
- ° Modal
- ° Popover and popup
- ° Spinner

- Miscellaneous components

We will learn about the usage and examples of each of the mentioned components.

Ionic CSS components

Mobile Apps are required to provide an engaging user experience. The styles and look and feel are represented by CSS in a Hybrid Mobile App. It takes a lot of time for a developer to write the CSS styles for multiple device screen sizes and so many UI elements. Ionic Framework provides reusable CSS styles that help developers in creating awesome Mobile Apps and decrease the development time rapidly. We will be discussing different CSS styles available for developers to use and customize.

Header

The header corresponds to the static and fixed region on the top of the screen, which can contain a title in the center and buttons on the left or right. Headers have their own CSS class and also for showing different header colors. For example:

```
<div class='bar bar-header bar-{color}'>
  <h1 class='title'> Header </h1>
</div>
```

We can replace {color} with the color themes available in Ionic, for example, light, stable, positive, calm, balanced, energized, assertive, royal, or dark. There is another class to display a sub header too, along with the header:

```
<div class='bar bar-subheader'>
  <h2 class='title'>Sub Header</h2>
</div>
```

We should remember to use the CSS class that has subheader to the <ion-content> directive.

Footer

Footer classes are exactly similar to headers in that they have the class `bar-footer` for the footer and `bar-{color}` representing a specific color for the footer. If we want to place buttons in the header or footer, we can place them before or after the title in HTML code according to where we want them to appear:

```
<div class="bar bar-footer">
  <button class="button">Home</button>
  <div class="title">Title</div>
  <button class="button">Login</button>
</div>
```

Buttons

Buttons are an important part of the UI as they drive actions in the whole Mobile App's UI. Ionic provides a variety of CSS styling options to display different buttons. Ionic has the class `button` for styling any button and has all the default colors that are available to headers/footers. The CSS class for any color would be `button-{color}` where color can be replaced by `balanced`, `assertive`, `calm`, and so on. The following image shows different sized buttons using all color themes:

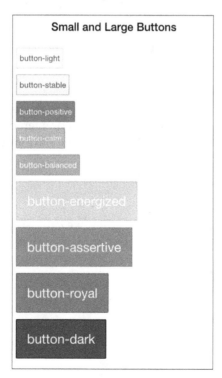

Buttons can be of different sizes too. There are two classes, button-large and button-small, that provide two variances for having a larger button than normal and a smaller button than normal, respectively. If we want to create full-width buttons for Mobile Apps, there are two CSS classes. The button-block applies the display: block CSS property and allows the button to take 100% of its parent width. If we add the button-full CSS class to a button, then the button would stretch across the entire width and would not have left or right borders.

If we want to show buttons with an outline only, then we can use the CSS class button-outline. The background color is transparent for this CSS class. Also, the outline color and text color are the same as the color class used on the button.

In order to show a button without a background or a border, the button-clear CSS class can be used.

Icon buttons

Icons can be added to any buttons by using built-in icons called **Ionicons** (http://ionicons.com) or any custom font pack. Icons can also be set as a child element to the button element:

```
<button class="button">
  <i class="icon ion-home"></i>
</button>
<button class="button icon-left ion-settings">
  Text
</button>
```

We can decide the alignment of the icon by using the classes icon-left or icon-right. Icons can be put directly on a button or even on a link tag given button class and icon class along with it. The same buttons can be used in the header or footer too.

Button bar

If we want to group multiple buttons together, we can use this CSS class for creating a bar of buttons. The CSS class to be used is button-bar and the usage is as follows:

```
<div class="button-bar">
  <a class="button button-balanced icon-left ion-home">Home</a>
  <a class="button button-calm icon-left ion-
    settings">Settings</a>
```

```
    <a class="button button-assertive icon-left ion-chevron-
      right">Next</a>
</div>
```

A button bar can be added to the header or footer also.

Lists

Mobile views due to limited space cannot show big tables and grids. List is the most popular and widely used UI design pattern used for mobile views. The list contains a collection of list items, which can contain any content ranging from text, images, thumbnails, icons, and so on:

```
<ul class="list">
  <li class="item">
  </li>
</ul>
```

In Ionic Framework, there are CSS classes as well as directives for multi-featured lists. There are different classes to support dividers, icons, buttons, thumbnails, and so on.

List dividers

Apart from the list items, there can be dividers added to the list. There is a class, item-divider, that will appear to be dividing multiple list items:

```
<div class="list">
  <div class="item item-divider">
    Display Settings
  </div>
  <a class="item" href="#">
    Icons Display
  </a>
</div>
```

List icons

Generally, list items have mixed content and icons play an important role in highlighting any list item. The icons can be placed on either the left or right side. Icons can be chosen from the built-in Ionicons or any custom font pack chosen as a font. The class item-icon-left or item-icon-right has to be included for every item. If icons are required on both sides, both CSS classes can be used.

List buttons

A `<button>` element can also be placed on the left or right by adding the classes `item-button-left` and `item-button-right` respectively.

Item avatars or thumbnails

In order to display images on list items, the `item-avatar` or `item-thumbnail` classes can be used. An avatar is a smaller image that is rounded, and a thumbnail is a bigger picture generally in a square shape. The following code snippet shows examples for all the list item types:

```
<div class="list">
  <a class="item item-icon-left item-icon-right" href="#">
    <i class="icon ion-chatbubble-working"></i>
      Call Support
    <i class="icon ion-ios-telephone-outline"></i>
  </a>
  <a class="item item-avatar" href="#">
    <img src="user-avatar.jpg">
    <h2>Demo User</h2>
    <p>Bought 23 books since 2014.</p>
  </a>
  <a class="item item-thumbnail-left" href="#">
    <img src="book-cover.jpg">
    <h2>Bestseller Book</h2>
    <p>New Book</p>
  </a>
</div>
```

Cards

Cards is a new UI design pattern that has become popular on mobile screens as it makes it easy to segregate important information and content. Ionic provides special CSS classes to create strong mobile views. Cards create a box around the content and add a box shadow to it, as follows:

```
<div class="card">
  <div class="item item-text-wrap">
    Card dummy text content.
  </div>
</div>
```

Cards can also contain list items and the `list` class can be used along with the `card` class. Item dividers can be used in the cards to create distinguished content.

Forms

In order to display forms in Ionic, lists can be used to display a set of input controls or input items. Both the classes `item` and `item-input` should be used to display a user form element.

By default, the input elements take 100% width. For an input text element, you can add the classes on the `label` tag and use the placeholder property to simulate the input's label. When the user types some text, the placeholder gets hidden and is overridden by user input:

```
<label class="item item-input">
  <input type="text" placeholder="Dummy Text">
</label>
```

If you need to put a `label` and `input` tag in the same row, then put a new `span` element with the class `input-label` displaying the label on the left column of the item row:

```
<label class="item item-input">
  <span class="input-label">Name</span>
  <input type="text">
</label>
```

In order to stack labels on top of the `input` elements, use the class `item-floating-label` on the item row containing the `label` and the `input` element. Ionic has a special style for floating labels, which animate from being placeholders to stacked labels when the user starts typing in the `input` element.

As mentioned, the `input` elements take 100% width but if you want to have `inset` form elements then you can encapsulate a form list in a card or either add a class `list-inset` to the `list` element. If you want to inset only a single `input` element and not the entire list then use the class `item-input-inset` on the `item` element.

Input elements

Apart from standard `input` element tags there are other `input` elements such as `select box`, `checkbox`, `radio`, and so on, which can be used in forms on mobile views. Ionic provides various CSS styles for these input elements, which will be discussed here.

Checkbox

A checkbox in Ionic is similar to the HTML counterpart with a good and elegant UI. The class `item-checkbox` needs to be added to the container for the checkbox, and its label, the second class `checkbox`, is added to the label element:

```
<ul class="list">
  <li class="item item-checkbox">
  <label class="checkbox">
    <input type="checkbox">
  </label>
    Checkbox Option1
  </li>
</ul>
```

Radio button list

Similar to checkbox, if only a single option has to be selected out of a list, a radio button list control can be used. It will act in the same way as HTML `radio` input elements.

 The name for all the input-type `radio` elements should be the same.

The icon that will be shown on the right of the selected radio element can be defined in the HTML itself. Three CSS classes will be used for the radio list element, `item-radio` for the container, `item-content` for the label text to be shown, and `radio-icon` for the icon for the selected item:

```
<div class="list">
  <label class="item item-radio">
    <input type="radio" name="group">
    <div class="item-content">
      Radio Option 1
    </div>
    <i class="radio-icon ion-checkmark"></i>
  </label>
</div>
```

Toggle

A toggle control is a mobile-specific component used in lieu of a checkbox. It is more intuitive for mobile devices and provides a rich user experience. The code for the `toggle` elements requires a `checkbox` element wrapped in a label with the class `toggle`:

```
<div class="list">
  <li class="item item-toggle">
    <label class="toggle">
      <input type="checkbox">
      <div class="track">
        <div class="handle"></div>
      </div>
    </label>
  </li>
</div>
```

Range

The range control in Ionic is a slider to select a specific value. The `range` component can be applied to different color themes according to the Ionic themes:

```
<div class="item range">
  <i class="icon ion-volume-low"></i>
  <input type="range" name="volume">
  <i class="icon ion-volume-high"></i>
</div>
```

The range item will have a left-side icon, right-side icon, and an `input` element of type `range` in between.

Tabs

We have discussed the `tabs` component and directive in the previous chapters. We can also create tabs in other views by using CSS classes only. It is a horizontal bar present on the bottom of the view containing one or more tab items. The classes `tabs` are used on the container and the class `tab-item` for each item. Tabs can be given a color theme using the CSS classes such as `tabs-calm`, `tabs-assertive`, and so on:

```
<div class="tabs">
  <a class="tab-item">
    Tab 1
  </a>
```

```
      <a class="tab-item">
        Tab 2
      </a>
      <a class="tab-item">
        Tab 3
      </a>
    </div>
```

Tabs can also use some extra CSS classes to display icons and control their alignment. The list of those CSS classes has been discussed in *Chapter 4, Navigation and Routing in an Ionic App*, in the *Ionic Tabs* section.

Grid

In developing a UI, creating the layout is like laying the foundation, and a strong grid system helps create solid layouts. In Ionic Framework there is a CSS grid system, which is based on the CSS flexbox layout. It helps in automatically adjusting dynamic columns in a row or rows.

In Ionic we will use the `row` class to represent a row and the `col` class for a column. We can add as many as columns in a row ranging from 1 to n and they will adjust equally. By default, when we use the `col` class, equally spaced columns are created.

We can also explicitly define the size by using classes such as `col-50`, `col-33`, `col-75`, and so on, and the rest of the columns will adjust accordingly. We can also give offset to the columns by adding the keyword `offset` in the column `class` name, for example, `col-offset-50`, `col-offset`, and so on.

In order to align columns vertically among a row, we can use the CSS classes `col-top`, `col-center`, and `col-bottom` respectively. The columns can be made to stack in a specific screen size and become responsive by adding the CSS classes `responsive-sm`, `responsive-md`, or `responsive-lg` for a small screen size (smaller than landscape phone), medium (smaller than portrait tablet), or large (smaller than landscape tablet).

The example code for using a grid or column is:

```
    <div class="row">
      <div class="col col-50">.col.col-50</div>
      <div class="col">.col</div>
      <div class="col">.col</div>
    </div>
```

```
<div class="row">
  <div class="col col-75">.col.col-75</div>
  <div class="col">.col</div>
</div>

<div class="row">
  <div class="col">.col</div>
  <div class="col col-75">.col.col-75</div>
</div>

<div class="row">
  <div class="col">.col</div>
  <div class="col">.col</div>
</div>
```

Utility

There are some utility classes that can be used along with multiple components. Ionic Framework has standard colors that can be used throughout the Mobile App with other styles. Utility color styles can be customized and existing themes can be modified. You can modify color variables in the _variables.scss file.

Ionic also comes with an icon font set that contains the most common fonts. These can be used by applying the icon class name and the specific class for different icons. For example:

```
<i class="icon ion-email"></i>
```

Also, there are padding classes available to add a padding of 10px between the outer box and the inner content. The class padding adds padding to all sides of the element whereas other CSS classes can be used for giving padding on special sides.

For example, padding-vertical, padding-horizontal for top-bottom and left-right respectively and padding-top, padding-right, and padding-bottom, for respective sides.

Ionic JS components

CSS is used for styling mobile components but JavaScript is used to write logic and create the user experience in a Hybrid App. Ionic has reusable Angular directives that help developers create smooth mobile-specific experiences. Apart from directives, Ionic also has controllers and services in its library to help create mobile-specific components. We will be discussing the most important components in this section of the chapter.

Actionsheet – $ionicActionSheet

The `actionsheet` component is a sliding panel that comes from the bottom and can contain multiple buttons intended to perform some actions in the Mobile App. This component has been inspired from the `actionsheet` component in iOS. `$ionicActionSheet` is a service in Ionic Library that can be injected in any controller and initiated using the `show` method.

The `show` method inputs a set of options mentioned in the following table to control the `actionsheet` component.

 A new isolated scope is created when the `show` method is called.

Name	Type	Description
buttons	[Object]	If extra buttons need to be shown, passed as array of objects. Each object can contain a `text` property.
titleText	String	Text for the title of Actionsheet.
cancelText	String	Text shown for a cancel button.
destructiveText	String	Text shown for a destructive button.
buttonClicked	Function	Callback called when any extra button is clicked.
cancel	Function	Callback called on click of cancel button.
destructiveButtonClicked	Function	Callback function for a destructive button.
cancelOnStateChange	Boolean	Value to define whether to cancel actionsheet on state change.
cssClass	String	Custom CSS class applied on actionsheet.

The code for an example is as follows:

```
// Action Sheet Initialization using Properties
var sheetId = $ionicActionSheet.show({
  titleText: 'Manage Books',
  buttons: [ { text: '<b>Add New Book </b>' } ],
  cancelText: 'Cancel',
```

```
    destructiveText: 'Delete Book',
    cancel: function() {
      // code when cancel button is clicked
    },
    buttonClicked: function(index) {
      //  code which is to be executed on button click
    }
});
```

Backdrop - $ionicBackdrop

A backdrop is a transparent blackish UI screen that appears behind popups, loading, and other overlays. Multiple UI components require a backdrop, but only one backdrop appears in DOM. In order to use a backdrop, any component can call the `retain` method, and whenever its usage is over the component can call the `release` method.

The code for demonstrating its usage is as follows:

```
$stateProvider.state('homeView',{
  //Show a backdrop for one second
  $scope.action = function() {
    $ionicBackdrop.retain();
    $timeout(function() {
      $ionicBackdrop.release();
    }, 1000);
  };
});
```

Form inputs

Apart from the normal input elements to take text format inputs, there are special form input directives for checkboxes, radio, and toggle. We have already discussed the CSS styles used for the same, but you can use directives themselves to achieve the functionality along with the style.

The <ion-checkbox> directive

This directive adds the required styles to a checkbox. It renders like a normal angular checkbox:

```
ion-checkbox ng-model="isChecked">Checkbox Label</ion-checkbox>
```

The <ion-radio> directive

The `<ion-radio>` directive is also used to style the radio input according to the mobile UI. In order to create a set of radio buttons, please give the same `ng-model` property to all and use `ng-value` to assign a value for a specific radio element:

```
<ion-radio ng-model="option" ng-value="'1'">Option 1</ion-radio>
<ion-radio ng-model="option" ng-value="'2'">Option 2</ion-radio>
```

The <ion-toggle> directive

This directive creates a toggle switch that can manipulate a boolean model:

```
<ion-toggle ng-model="isOpen" toggle-class='toggle-calm'>Open
Drawer</ion-checkbox>
```

Gestures and events

In a Mobile App, gestures and events are very important in shaping the user experience. The event handling should be perfect and there should be a multitude of events available to developers for adding appropriate actions for different events. In Ionic Framework, there are different event directives that can be used to bind callbacks for those events. Also, there is an `$ionicGesture` service that can be used to programmatically bind the events with callbacks.

The $ionicGesture service

The methods available under the `$ionicGesture` service are given as follows.

The on method

It adds an event listener for a gesture on an element. The signature for the method is as follows:

```
on(eventType,callback,$element,options)
```

The following table lists the details of each argument:

Param	Type	Details
eventType	string	The gesture event to be registered
callback	function(e)	Event listener method to be called when event is triggered

Param	Type	Details
$element	element	Element on which the event is bound
options	object	Used to set extra options

The method returns an `ionic.Gesture` object, which is used to detach the event later.

The off method

It removes an event listener for a gesture on an element. The signature for the method is as follows:

```
off(gesture,eventType,callback)
```

The following table lists the details of each arguments:

Param	Type	Details
gesture	ionic.Gesture	The gesture that is to be removed
eventType	string	The gesture name that is to be removed
callback	function(e)	Callback that needs to be deregistered

Gesture events

A list of gesture events available in Ionic Framework are given in the following table:

Event name	Description
on-hold	It occurs when the touch stays for longer than 500 ms. Long touch events.
on-tap	It occurs when a quick touch is done on an element.
on-double-tap	It occurs on a double tap on a location.
on-touch	It is called immediately when the user starts a touch.
on-release	It is called when the user ends a touch.
on-drag	It is called when one touch is moved around the page. If dragging is allowed, scrolling should be disabled.
on-drag-up	It is called when element is dragged up.
on-drag-right	It is called when an element is dragged right.

Event name	Description
on-drag-left	It is called when an element is dragged left.
on-drag-down	It is called when an element is dragged down.
on-swipe	It is called when a touch moves at high speed in any direction.
on-swipe-up	It is called when a touch moves at high speed moving up.
on-swipe-right	It is called when a touch moves at high speed moving right.
on-swipe-left	It is called when a touch moves at high speed moving left.
on-swipe-down	It is called when a touch moves at high speed moving down.

Lists

List is the most popular component used in any Mobile App. Generally, all the data displayed in a mobile view is in the form of a list. A list can have multiple list items representing rows. A list item can contain any content ranging from text to icons and custom elements.

The <ion-list> directive

This directive represents a list in Ionic Framework. This directive supports complex interactions such as drag to reorder, swipe to edit, and removing items. The <ion-list> directive can consist of one or more <ion-item> directives representing each row. There are other directives augmenting its functionality such as <ion-option-button> used for swipe to edit buttons, <ion-reorder-button> shown while reorder is enabled, and <ion-delete-button> shown while deleting a row item.

The attributes available for this directive are given in the following table:

Attribute (all optional)	Type	Details
delegate-handle	string	The handle used for passing the reference of the list with the object $ionicListDelegate
type	string	Type of list used (options: list-inset or card)
show-delete	boolean	Whether to show delete buttons or hide them
show-reorder	boolean	Whether to show reordering buttons or hide them
can-swipe	boolean	Whether to allow swiping of the list to show option buttons

The following code explains the usage :

```
// Example with complex Scenario
<ion-list ng-controller="AppCtrl"
show-delete="shouldShowDelete"
show-reorder="shouldShowReorder"
can-swipe="listCanSwipe">
  <ion-item ng-repeat="row in rows" class="item-thumbnail-left">
    <h2>{{item.title}}</h2>
    <p>{{item.description}}</p>
    <ion-option-button class="button-positive" ng-
      click="share(item)">
      Share
    </ion-option-button>
    <ion-option-button class="button-info" ng-click="edit(item)">
      Edit
    </ion-option-button>
    <ion-delete-button class="ion-minus-circled" ng-
      click="items.splice($index, 1)">
    </ion-delete-button>
    <ion-reorder-button class="ion-navicon" on-
      reorder="reorderItem(item, $fromIndex, $toIndex)">
    </ion-reorder-button>
  </ion-item>
</ion-list>
```

Loading – $ionicLoading

`$ionicLoading` is an angular service that controls the display of an overlay representing a loader. The loading indicator can be configured by passing certain options to the `show` method of this service.

The following is the usage of this service:

```
// Sample Module
angular.module('MyApp', ['ionic'])
controller('MyCtrl', function($scope, $ionicLoading) {
  $scope.show = function() {
    $ionicLoading.show({
      template: 'Loading...'
    });
  };
  $scope.hide = function(){
    $ionicLoading.hide();
  };
});
```

The important options available to be passed to the show method are:

Field	Type	Details
template	string	HTML content of the indicator
templateUrl	string	Template URL for the HTML content of the indicator
scope	object	The scope to be a child of
noBackdrop	boolean	Whether to hide the translucent backdrop
hideOnStateChange	boolean	Whether to hide the loader during state change
delay	number	Delay (in ms) to show the indicator
duration	number	Time (in ms) after which the indicator will be hidden

Modal – $ionicModal

This is a service that controls displaying a popup over the existing UI temporarily. It uses the `<ion-modal-view>` directive in its template to represent the modal DOM element. It is used for generally editing an item or showing a dialog box or a choice box. There are two methods available on the `$ionicModal` service, `fromTemplate` and `fromTemplateUrl`, which takes input as `template string` or `template url` respectively as a first parameter. The second argument to both methods is the `options` object, which is passed to the initialize method of the `IonicModal` controller instance.

The IonicModal controller

This is a controller instantiated by the `$ionicModal` service. The `ionicModal` method `remove` should be called after the use of the modal is over in order to avoid memory leaks.

The different methods available to this controller are as follows.

initialize(options)

It creates a new modal controller instance. It takes as an argument an `options` object, which should contain the following properties:

- `scope (object)`: The scope to be a child of.
- `animation (string)`: The animation to show and hide. The default is `slide-in-up`.
- `focusFirstInput (boolean)`: The control whether to focus first input in modal or not.
- `backdropClickToClose (boolean)`: Whether to close modal on clicking backdrop.
- `hardwareBackButtonClose (boolean)`: The control to decide whether modal should be closed using hardware back button or not.
- `show()`: This method is used to show the modal instance.
- `hide()`: This method is used to hide the modal instance.
- `remove()`: This method is used to remove the modal instance from memory.
- `isShown()`: This method returns a boolean representing whether the modal is shown or not.

Popover – $ionicPopover

A Popover component is also modeled similarly to modal and has two objects, the $ionicPopover service and the ionicPopover controller. Popover is a view that floats above the app's content. Popover can be used to display extra information or take input for a choice. The content of a Popover needs to be put inside an <ion-popover-view> element.

The $ionicPopover service exposes similar methods such as the $ionicModal service — fromTemplate and fromTemplateUrl. The ionicPopover controller also has similar events to the ionicModal controller. The initialize method for this controller has the options object as input but it does not contain the property animation.

Spinner – ion-spinner

In a mobile UI or views, only a particular section of view needs to be refreshed or loaded and a spinner/loader needs to be displayed in that section. <ion-spinner> is a directive that displays loader icons. There are multiple available icons such as spiral, ripple, dots, lines, and so on. The theme colors for Ionic can also be used along with using class names such as spinner-<theme>.

The following is the usage of this directive:

```
<ion-spinner icon="spiral spinner-calm"></ion-spinner>
```

Miscellaneous components

There are some extra utility and miscellaneous components available in Ionic Framework. The components can be in the form of directives or services.

$ionicPosition

It is a utility service used to retrieve the position of DOM elements. This can be used to position elements absolutely over the screen. It has two methods available, position and offset, which fetch the position relative to its parent or relative to the document respectively. The methods return an object containing the properties top, left, width, and height.

$ionicConfigProvider

Ionic has a lot of default configurations and styles for different platforms. For example, in iOS, the tab bar is shown below by default, and in Android, the tab bar is shown on top. The Ionic platform exposes a provider to manage these configurations, which is called $ionicConfigProvider. This provider can be used during the config phase of your Angular app. The configuration is, by default, set for the specific platform.

The following is the usage of this variable:

```
var myApp = angular.module('MyApp', ['ionic']);
myApp.config(function($ionicConfigProvider) {
  $ionicConfigProvider.views.maxCache(5);
  $ionicConfigProvider.backButton.text('Go Back').icon('ion-
    chevron-left');
});
```

A list of different configurations that can be set using this provider are as follows:

- `views.transition(transition)`: Animation style while viewing transitions
- `scrolling.jsScrolling(booleanValue)`: Setting usage for native JS scrolling or not
- `backButton.icon(value)`: Setting the back button icon
- `backButton.text(value)`: Setting the text for back button
- `tabs.position(value)`: Setting the position of tabs out of top or bottom
- `navBar.alignTitle(value)`: Setting the alignment side for the navbar's title
- `spinner.icon(value)`: Setting the default icon for the spinner

Summary

In this chapter we have seen most of the components available in Ionic Framework as directives and services to build excellent Hybrid Mobile Apps. These components cover most of the use cases required for developing Mobile Apps. We have learnt about different CSS styles that can be used to create an engaging user experience in your Ionic Apps. Ionic Library also has JS components that we have discussed in detail in this chapter. We can also mix and match these components to build more complex directives. In the next chapter we will learn how we can integrate our apps with any web service or backend service providers.

6
Integrating App with Backend Services

Mobile Apps are incomplete without data, and the data on the mobile is not enough. We have learnt to start Mobile App projects and create complex views with different components. In this chapter we will learn how to integrate our Ionic Apps with web services to fetch and submit data. Use cases involving data exchange for Mobile Apps include central user authentication/authorization, saving your personalization data, storing images, searching public datasets, storing transactions, and so on. Mobile Apps have become a major source for collaboration and require strong integration to robust backend services to support communication and real-time messaging.

Here, we will first learn about the low-level constructs available in Angular/Ionic to integrate into any web service conforming to JSON/REST standards. There is also another object available that maps to REST entities directly, helping to shorten the integration development effort and time. The topics that will be discussed in this chapter are as follows:

- $http services
- Ionic services versus factories
- $resource and REST API
- Demystifying mBaaS
- Integrating with Parse
- Integrating with Firebase

Mobile Apps become meaningful with data, and to empower our Ionic Apps with data we need to have strong backend servers or APIs. We will discuss some cloud-based backends as a service solution, which are super easy to use with our Ionic Apps with minimal effort.

$http services

In web technologies, the best way to interact with any web service is through Ajax requests. As Ionic Framework is a Hybrid Mobile framework based on web technologies, it utilizes the power of Ajax to wire up Ionic Apps with any web services.

$http is an in-built Angular service that is used as an abstraction for native JavaScript Ajax calls. The $http service has some high-level methods exposed to make HTTP requests using different HTTP methods such as POST, GET, PUT, and so on.

There are different signatures for different methods, but the response for all the methods is exactly the same. All the methods in the $http service are based on the promise objects, which help in registering success and error callbacks that receive data at a later point in time as these requests are asynchronous in nature.

The two most important methods are .get and .post whose usage is as follows:

```
$http.get('/api/url/resource')
.then(function(response){
  // this is success callback
},function(errorResponse) {
  // this is error callback
});
```

The GET request method takes only one argument, the URL for the request, and registers two callbacks with the method of the promise object returned:

```
$http.post('/api/url/resource',{data:'custom data'})
.then(function(response){
  // this is success callback
},function(errorResponse) {
  // this is error callback
});
```

The POST request method takes two arguments, the URL for the request and the data to be sent in the body of the post request.

The other methods available that have a signature exactly like the GET method are as follows:

* $http.put
* $http.head
* $http.delete
* $http.jsonp
* $http.patch

There are default headers sent along with each HTTP request. Some web services require us to send custom headers for authorization or content-type for which the $http service exposes a provider to set custom default headers. We can use the provider to set up default headers in the config phase of the Ionic App. We can also use the $http object to set default headers in the run block or any controller/service:

```
module.config(function($http) {
    $http.defaults.headers.common.Content-Type = 'application/json';
});
module.run(function($http) {
    $http.defaults.headers.post.Authorization = 'Basic sdkJKHSmd'
});
```

The response object

The response object passed as an argument to the callback functions contains the following properties:

Name	Type	Description
data	String/ Object	Response body received in the Ajax request, generally JSON is parsed.
status	Number	HTTP status code returned by the request.
headers	Function	Header getter function.
config	Object	The configuration object used to generate the request.
statusText	String	HTTP status text for the response.

The response object can be used to extract the data sent by the server and process it.

The $http constructor method

Another way to make an Ajax request is by using the $http constructor method and passing the request configuration object directly. For example:

```
var req = {
  method: 'POST',
  url: '/api/url/resource',
  headers: {
    'Content-Type': 'plain/text'
```

```
    },
    data: { objectName: 'Value' },
    cache: true
  }
$http(req).then(function(){...}, function(){...});
```

The $http service also supports caching by passing the cache property to the configuration object and setting it to true. Angular stores the response temporarily to the $cacheFactory object and serves the same request with a response from there.

Ionic services vs factories

Services/factories in Ionic are used to abstract common business logic and integration to the backend services. A data access layer and business logic layer can be implemented using Ionic service or factory. Ionic service or factory can be used interchangeably and are available as a method on the angular.module object.

 Generally, a service is used to represent the data access layer whereas a factory is used to implement the entity layer or business logic layer. Both objects are singleton in nature, meaning only once instance is created throughout the app's life cycle, which is shared between multiple controllers or other angular modules.

We will take the example of our BookStore App to create an authentication service for it, and a booksFactory with factory object.

Ionic service – authentication service

Ionic service is a special Angular construct that represents an object created using a constructor pattern, exposing certain methods abstracting app logic or integrating with the backend. Services can be injected into any module using **Dependency Injection (DI)** but its instance is created only once. Service is lazily instantiated only when any component that depends on it comes into focus. There are multiple in-built utility services such as $http, $timeout, and so on which can be used throughout the app.

A service is created using the .service() method available on the angular.module object. The first argument needs to be the name of the service and the second argument is the dependency injection array, which has the names of all dependencies, and the last element is the constructor function.

The following code explains the usage of this service:

```
angular.module('module.services',[])
.service('ServiceName',
  ['dependency1','dependency2',
    function(dependency1,dependency2) {
      this.variable1 = 1 //default value
      this.variable2 = 3 //default value
      this.method1 = function() {
        return binaryOp(this.variable1,this.variable2);
        //binaryOp can be any local method
      }
    }
  ]
);
```

We can model our BookStore sample app's authentication service using this construct. We will expose four given methods to this service as follows:

- signup: A method used to sign up a new user, taking input as a user object

- login: A method to log in a user and save sessionToken to cookies

- logout: A method to log a user out of a web service and remove the sessionToken argument

Here is the code sample for defining a service:

```
angular.module('BookStore.Services',[])
.service('UserAuth',
  ['$http','$cookies',
    function($http,$cookies) {
      this.baseApiUrl = 'http://localhost:9000/api'; // Sample
        URL to be replaced by your own API url
      this.signup = function(userObj) {
        // Making a POST $http call to /signup API call
        return $http.post(this.baseApiUrl+'/signup',userObj)
      }
      this.login = function(username,password) {
        // Making a GET $http call to /login API call
        return $http.get(this.baseApiUrl+'/login?username='+username+
          '&password='+password)
        .then(function(response) {
          if(response.data.loginSuccessful == 'true')
          {
            $cookies.put('sessionToken',response.data.sessionToken);
          }
        });
```

```
        }
        this.logout = function() {
          // Making a GET $http call to /logout API call
          return $http.post(this.baseApiUrl+'/
          logout?sessionToken='+$cookies.get('sessionToken'))
          .then(function(response){
            $cookies.remove('sessionToken');
          });
        }
      }
    }
  ]);
```

Ionic factory – BooksFactory

Ionic Factory is very similar to service and can be used interchangeably with it. The only syntactical difference is that it returns an object exposing selective methods, which can be called to use the service. It is also based on a singleton pattern and the same instance is shared between different modules.

The service or factory can be used by injecting it into any controller or other service, and calling the exposed methods passing required parameters. We can use this to create a factory pattern for our app using it to manage entities or objects.

The following code explains the usage of this service:

```
angular.module('module.services', [])
.factory('ObjectFactory',
  ['dependency1','dependency2',
    function(dependency1,dependency2) {
      this.objectsArray = [] //load array from server
      this.getObjects = function() {
        return this.objectsArray;
      }
    }
  ]
);
.controller('ConsumerCtrl',['ObjectFactory',
function(ObjectFactory) {
  $scope.objects = ObjectFactory.getObjects();
}]);
```

We can create a BooksFactory factory to implement logic regarding managing book entities in our app. We can expose the methods that can be used by multiple views or controllers. We will be exposing the following methods:

- getBooks: A method that can be used to get a list of books to be displayed. Certain optional arguments can be passed to the method to filter the results:
    - Category: Fetch books related to that category
    - Author: Fetch books for a specific author
    - SortBy: Pass the field according to which list should be sorted

- getBookDetails: Passing a specific book ID to get all the details regarding that book.

- addToFavorite: Adding a book to your favorites.

Here is the code sample for defining a service:

```
angular.module('BookStore.Services',[])
.factory('BooksFactory',
  ['$http',
    function($http) {
      var baseApiUrl = 'http://localhost:9000/api'; // Sample URL
        to be replaced by your own API url
      var booksList = [];
      var favoriteBooks = [];
      var getBooks = function(category,author,sortBy) {
        var filters = {};
        if(category)
          filters['category'] = category;
        if(author)
          filters['author'] = author;
        if(category)
          filters['sortBy'] = sortBy;
        // Making a POST $http call to /signup API call
        return $http.post(baseApiUrl+'/books',filters)
      }
      var getBookDetails = function(bookId) {
        // Making a GET $http call to /books/:id API call
        return $http.get(baseApiUrl+'/books/'+bookId);
      }
      var addToFavorite = function(bookObj) {
        if(bookObj) {
          favoriteBooks.push(bookObj);
          return true;
        }
      }
```

```
        return { getBooks: getBooks,
          getBookDetails: getBookDetails
          addToFavorite: addToFavorite
        }
      }
    ]
  );
```

$resource and REST API

REST is becoming the most popular choice of design pattern for the latest web services being developed. All new platforms, frameworks, and programming languages support REST standards out of the box. REST interfaces usually involve a collection of resources with identifiers, and supporting different actions using all HTTP verbs. For example, GET requests to a /users/ resource would fetch a list of users, and POST requests to /users/ can be used to create a new user. The identifier can be used in a GET request to the URL /users/john to fetch a specific user object with a unique identifier john.

$resource is an in-built factory that helps create a local resource object that integrates with the REST API implicitly. The resource object has in-built methods representing common methods such as save, get, delete, and so on. These methods internally interact with the API URL using the $http object. $resource is available only after injecting the ngResource module.

The signature for the $resource service constructor is as follows:

$resource(url, [paramDefaults], [actions], options);

The url argument can contain dynamic parameters represented by names starting from the ':' symbol. The second argument defines the default values for the dynamic parameters expected in url. The third argument, actions, is used to map new actions to custom url. This object can contain one or multiple action fields defined by objects having properties such as method, params, url, isArray, and many more. The $resource constructor when executed returns the object that contains the methods exposed, such as $save, $get, and so on, used to perform CRUD.

The following is the code example:

```
var Book = $resource('/book/:bookId', {bookId:'@id'});
var books = Book.query(function(){
  //books var get filled with books list from server
});
Book.get({bookId:123}, function(book) {
```

```
    book.isNew = true;
    book.$save();
});
```

Demystifying mBaaS

More and more Mobile Apps are being developed at every passing second, but they also die out as fast as they appear. The average life of an app on the mobile of a user is just three months. If we spend a lot of money and effort in developing a backend for every app including the REST API, authentication service, login service, and so on, it is not justified. The mobile backend needs special services such as a multi-platform Push Notification service, analytics service, logging service, and so on. It is very tedious to develop these for each and every app you make, so certain IT companies started providing mobile backends as a service on the cloud.

The mBaaS services connect the cloud storage to Mobile Apps using custom SDKs or REST APIs. They also provide supplementary services such as Push Notification services, User Management, Social Networking services, and so on. A few popular mBaaS services are:

- **Parse**: Facebook acquired mBaaS providing JS SDK, which can be used with Hybrid Apps

- **Firebase**: Google acquired mBaaS specializing in real-time APIs for use cases such as chat, news stream, and so on

- **Azure Mobile Services**: mBaaS by Microsoft on the popular cloud platform Azure

- **Kinvey**: One of the most mature and old mBaaS providing SDKs for all platforms

- **Anypresence**: Popular mBaaS providing the code for the backend to enable enterprise-level customization

We will be discussing only two out of this list, Parse and Firebase.

Integrating with Parse

Parse has evolved from being a simple cloud backend to a sophisticated platform having a multitude of features. Parse is maintained by Facebook itself and has excellent integration with all Facebook SDKs.

Parse has segmented its platform into three major sections:

- **Core**: APIs to store and retrieve data, user management, and webhooks for writing custom logic on the cloud
- **Push**: Services enabling the management of Push Notifications for multiple platforms
- **Analytics**: Tracking any data or events for your app and users in real time

Discussion on all of these services is beyond the scope of this book, but we will explain how you can integrate Parse into your enables and leverage the platform.

The high-level steps involved in integrating your Ionic App will be discussed here.

Step 1 – creating an app on Parse

In order to create an app on Parse, one requires to sign up for the account on www. parse.com. The basic account is absolutely free and provides sufficient storage and bandwidth for a prototype or the initial phase of any app. After registering on Parse, log in to your account and create a new app by giving its name as shown in the following screenshot:

Step 2 – getting API keys

In order to get API keys that will be used to integrate SDK or REST, the API needs to be obtained from the console. After logging in to the Parse console and selecting the appropriate app on the top left, go to the **Settings** page from the top menu.

On the **Settings** page there is a menu on the left where an option for **Keys** needs to be selected. This view will contain all the keys—**REST API Key**, **App ID**, **Client Key**, and **JavaScript Key**. The important keys for us are the **REST API Key**, **App ID**, and **JavaScript Key**. These keys can be used while integrating with the Ionic App.

Step 3 – configuring appropriate settings

In the same view, other important settings can be configured, for example, all the settings regarding user authentication such as using username and password authentication or social authentication. We can also set email settings such as reply-to email address, or define mail templates to be sent on sign up, or password reset.

The settings related to Push Notifications can be configured using the **Push** menu option on the left.

Step 4 – integrating SDK or integrating using REST API

We will be discussing two ways in which we can integrate with Parse, either using the SDK or using the REST API directly.

Using SDK – downloading and overview

Parse has SDKs available for each native mobile platform, iOS, Android, and Windows phone. It has SDKs for other programming languages and platforms such as PHP, OS X, Windows, .NET, Arduino, and so on. We would require only the JS SDK as we are developing a Hybrid App using JS only. The JS SDK can be downloaded from `https://parse.com/docs/downloads`.

The JS SDK is based on backbone-styled collections. The SDK does not require any external libraries and is a collection of JavaScript objects and methods. The main objects are `Parse.Object` and `Parse.User`, which are used with multiple methods. The SDK contains functionality to query data from the server, create data, upload binary files, authenticate users, and call custom server code too. The JS key needs to be set or intialized in the `run` block of our Ionic App.

The custom code written on the server is called Cloud Code and is written using JavaScript too. Most of the node modules can also be used in your Cloud Code. The Cloud Code methods can be called using the JS SDK and REST API too. The JS SDK calls can be abstracted using Ionic Services defined earlier in this chapter.

The detailed guide for the JS SDK is available at `https://parse.com/docs/js/guide`.

Using REST API

The REST API can be integrated easily if we do not want to learn about the JS SDK. The API follows many standards and can be used with Ionic `$resource` discussed in this chapter. REST API calls can also be made using a normal `$http` object and abstracted using Ionic services/factories.

Along with the REST API calls, the **Application ID Key** and **REST API Key** need to be sent as the custom headers **X-Parse-Application-Id** and **X-Parse-REST-API-Key**.

We can make API calls to in-built objects such as Users, Roles, Sessions, Files, Cloud Functions, and Push Notifications using the URLs `/1/<objectName>/:<objectId>` and different HTTP verbs to perform create, read, update, or delete operations.

We can use the **Core** option on the top menu and sub menu **Data** to add a class and then add rows. These classes can be managed using the URLs `/1/classes/<className>/:<objectId>` with different HTTP verbs such as `GET` for getting a list of objects, `POST` to create a new single object, `PUT` to update specific objects, `GET` along with object id to get details for specific objects, and `DELETE` for deleting specific objects. These API URLs are perfect for using with the `$resource` object as they follow REST principles. To get more details, please use the URL `https://parse.com/docs/rest/guide`.

Integrating to Firebase

Firebase storage specializes in real-time communication. Firebase is best suitable for use cases such as chatting, news stream, collaboration apps, and so on. It also provides user management services and integration to social APIs.

Firebase stores the database in JSON format and maintains a single version only, which is synced for all the clients connected to it. The Firebase SDKs ensure syncing the clients and managing data locking. It even works offline and records your operations offline to be synced online later.

Few important facts about the firebase are as follows:

- Firebase authentication is a set of features that enable your Mobile Apps to be authenticated using SDKs only. It supports standard user- and password-based authentication as well as social auth integrations with Facebook, Twitter, Github, and Google.

- Firebase Hosting enables you to host your web apps also on Firebase's production grade cloud servers and are SSL-enabled.

- Firebase also has a JS SDK and REST API that can be used to integrate to the Ionic App in a similar way with Parse. The URL for the JS SDK is `https://www.firebase.com/docs/web/api/`. The detailed documentation for integrating the Firebase REST API can be found at `https://www.firebase.com/docs/rest/api/`.

Summary

We have finally learned how to integrate our Ionic App with any backend and add life to our app. Ionic App will be enabled now to fetch and store data from any custom-made web service or easy-to-use mBaaS available on the market. We have seen how to create Ionic services and use them in multiple views or controllers. MbaaS seems to be a perfect choice for wiring up a quick backend to your Ionic App. Firebase and Parse are the recommended mBaaS with wide community support. In the next chapter we will learn about testing our app on real devices.

Testing App on Real Devices

7

We have learnt how to develop Mobile Apps for multiple platforms and devices using Ionic Framework, but we cannot launch it unless we test it. During the development also, we should test our apps on actual devices so that we can validate the functional aspects of our app. The Mobile App will behave differently on various platforms and screen sizes and hence it is necessary to check the output on most of the popular devices.

In this chapter, we will learn how to run our apps on actual devices using different approaches. We have already seen how we test our Ionic Apps in the browser during development. We will also briefly discuss the special provision in our browsers to emulate actual devices and test our app on tens of options without the need of getting the physical devices. An individual developer cannot easily get hold of all devices such as an iPhone, Nexus, iPad, Galaxy, or Windows Tab/Phone. So, I would recommend using the option of testing your Ionic App on all the emulator types available in the browser.

But generally, as developers are very fond of devices, they might end up having or arranging one device per platform. We will be discussing different platforms and methods to test your app on real devices. The following topics will be covered in this chapter:

- Testing on browser emulators
- Ionic view app
- Making a debug build
- Remote debugging
- Testing using Ngrok

It is important to build our apps bug-free so that they are readily accepted by public app stores such as Google Play and the Apple app store. At the end of this chapter, we will briefly describe the procedure for submitting the builds of your Ionic App to these app stores.

Testing on browser emulators

It is so blissful if we can test our Ionic App on different platforms and screen sizes without the hassle of deploying and installing it several times. Google Chrome, the most popular browser, has released a new device mode in their developer tools console from version 32 and above in the browser itself.

The device mode enables the developer to test any web URL on multiple screen sizes and platforms as Chrome emulates the browser userAgent, screen size, and resolutions. It also allows us to analyze the site performance on different network speeds by changing the throttle or network speed used for accessing that specific site. We can also simulate other device inputs such as touch, geolocation, and device orientation.

Overview of device mode in Chrome dev tools

In order to access all the emulators we need to start the device mode from the Chrome dev tools. Opening dev tools can be done either by going to the **Chrome** menu on the top right and selecting the **Tools | Developer Tools** option or we can right-click on any page element and select **Inspect Element**.

The keyboard shortcuts for opening dev tools are *F12*, *Ctrl + Shift + I* for Windows and *Cmd + Opt + I* for Mac machines. After opening the Chrome dev tools, you have to click on the device icon to turn on the **Device Mode**. When the **Device Mode** is turned on, the icon will turn blue, as shown in the following screenshot:

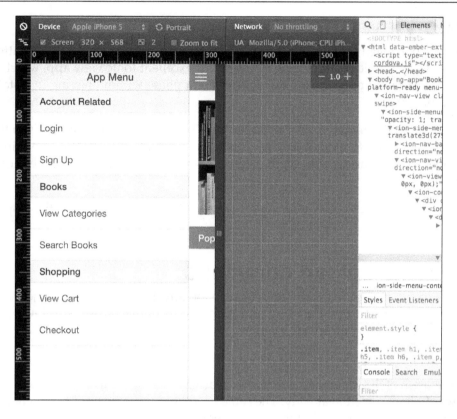

On the top left, you can set the device presets. There is a drop-down menu to select the device that you want to emulate. It has a multitude of options with existing devices from popular manufacturers such as Samsung, Sony, LG, Apple, and so on. If you select a particular device, the appropriate user agent is automatically selected, touch emulation is enabled, and the screen size and resolution are set. You can also change the screen size to emulate any custom device. There is another interesting option of **Network** for network throttling. The default option selected for this drop-down is **No throttling**, which can be changed to any network speed ranging from GPRS (50 KBPS) to Wi-Fi (30 MBPS). This option can also help you test your Ionic App for offline use cases.

This tool can only be used for basic testing as it has limitations such as GPU/CPU behavior is not emulated, the device browser UI for native elements is not emulated, and system displays such as address bar are not shown. It is therefore very important to test your app on actual devices, which we will learn about in the next sections.

Ionic view app

It can be a herculean task to set up the development environments for each platform and build apps. Ionic creators have released this excellent Ionic view app, which can be used to test your apps during the development phase without having to install it every time.

Ionic view app is integrated with the Ionic CLI. There are simple commands in the CLI that enable you to upload the app you are developing. This platform requires the developer to create an account on the `ionic.io` platform, which enables free access to this service.

The Ionic view app can be downloaded from the Google Play store and the Apple app store.

The Ionic upload command

In order to run the `upload` command, change the directory to the Ionic Project you want to upload. From the command prompt or terminal, type the following command in the same directory position:

```
ionic upload
```

The execution of this command will lead to a prompt asking for a username and password, if not signed in already. The same username and password that were used to sign up to the `ionic.io` platform will be required. After entering the credentials, the app will be uploaded to the cloud platform and the following output will be there:

```
RahatKhannaMachine:BookStore rahat.khanna$ ionic upload
No previous login existed. Attempting to log in now.

To continue, please login to your Ionic account.
Don't have one? Create a one at: https://apps.ionic.io/signup

Email: yehtechnologies@gmail.com
Password:
Logged in! :)
Uploading app....
Saved app_id, writing to ionic-core.js...
Successfully uploaded (f2ee313c)

Share your beautiful app with someone:

$ ionic share EMAIL

Saved api_key, writing to ionic-core.js...
```

The uploaded app can be shared with additional collaborators by using the
`ionic share <email>` command. The collaborators also need to have an
`ionic.io` command.

Viewing your app

After installing the Ionic view app from the public app stores, you would need to log
in using the `ionic.io` credentials. The Ionic view app has a default view to display
the list of apps uploaded to your account. It would show a gray shade for the app
that is in your account but not downloaded to the specific device, a blue shade for
the apps that are downloaded to the specific device, and a green shade for the app
that has been shared with you by someone else as shown in the following screenshot:

The Ionic view also supports Cordova device plugins such as SQLLite, Camera,
Device Motion, Barcode, and so on, and hence it is a perfect platform to test your
apps on actual devices easily. Once you have uploaded the app, you can update the
changes and test incremental versions as soon as you develop any new feature.

It also automatically detects platform-specific changes and renders your app
appropriately on iOS and Android devices. You can install it on multiple devices
and check it on different screen sizes.

Making debug build

While we can use the Ionic view app to see the output of our app and share the app with others to get feedback, but we cannot debug errors during the development on the actual app using this method.

We have to approach testing on actual devices by connecting our devices to development machines using USB and deploying debug builds to enable debugging. The process for making debug builds and running them on iOS and Android are different. We will discuss the method for both in this section.

Android debug build

In Android, the most basic step is to enable USB debugging in your Android device. The detailed steps are:

1. Enable the developer mode by going to **Settings | About Phone | Build number | Tap 7 times to become developer**.

2. After entering the developer mode you have to go to **Settings | Developer Options | USB Debugging**.

3. Now, you should connect your device to the development machine.

4. A dialog will appear on your device to allow the specific RSA key – **Please press the Ok button**. If you do not see this dialog, to ensure your system is connected, go to the `Android SDK tools` folder and type the command `adb devices`.

5. Now the device has been connected to the machine and enabled for debugging.

We will leverage the Ionic platform to make a debug build. Please go to the directory for your Ionic project. Please add Android and iOS using the `ionic platform add android ios` command. You can also use only a single platform name to add the respective platform separately. After the specific platforms are added, we can use the `ionic run [android|ios]` command to run our Ionic App on the specific device that is attached to our device. This will initiate the downloading of the required build dependencies for the first time, but from the next time, your build will be updated in your device instantly.

We will see the message **Launch Success** when the app is launched on your device, as follows:

```
BUILD SUCCESSFUL

Total time: 5.642 secs
Built the following apk(s):
    /Users/rahat.khanna/Documents/Hobby/Ionic/BookStore/platforms/andro
id/build/outputs/apk/android-debug.apk
Using apk: /Users/rahat.khanna/Documents/Hobby/Ionic/BookStore/platform
s/android/build/outputs/apk/android-debug.apk
Installing app on device...
Launching application...
LAUNCH SUCCESS
```

In order to see debug logs, please open Eclipse and Logcat or go to the `Android SDK` `platform-tools` folder and type in the commands `adb shell` and `logcat`.

iOS debug build

In iOS, making a debug build run on an actual device is a bit tricky. Apple has restrictions for installing and running apps on devices, which is managed by the Apple Developer Program. In order to run your app on an actual device you need to obtain a $99 annual fee license.

After buying an Apple Developer license, we need to obtain a provisioning profile. You have to sign in to the Apple Developer portal and create a developer provisioning profile. While you create a provisioning profile, you have to give a unique app ID (bundle identifier) for the app.

You have to install the provisioning profile after downloading it by double clicking on it. Go to the folder `platforms`, then to the `ios` folder and open the Xcode Project. Now, you should update the bundle identifier to match the id you used while creating the provisioning profile.

You can now use Xcode to select your device from the top panel and then click on the play (run) button. The Xcode should look like the following screenshot:

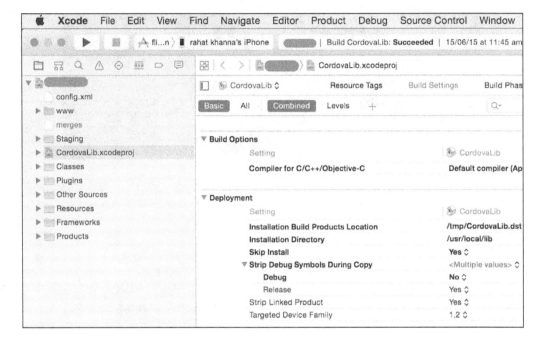

Remote debugging

There are times when the Mobile Apps being tested do not need to be connected to your development machine. Hybrid Apps mostly run JavaScript code, so the debugging is done mostly on the JS console. The remote debugging can be done using two ways, one using Chrome's remote web inspector tool and the other using a free tool called jsconsole.

Remote debugging using Chrome dev tools

Chrome enables a special remote debugging protocol for iOS and Android devices. It helps you see the logs remotely for your Ionic App running in a browser or as an app on your devices. In Android, the remote debugging is enabled for Chrome and also WebViews in apps. In iOS, remote debugging is enabled for your Ionic App running in Safari.

Android debugging

The basic requirements are Chrome 32 or later on the development machine, a USB cable to connect to the machine, and the latest Chrome for Android on the device itself. The steps to be followed are given here:

- USB debugging should be enabled on your device
- In order to discover a device on desktop Chrome, open the URL `chrome://inspect` on the desktop browser and check the **Discover USB devices** option
- Every connected device will be shown with its open tabs
- In order to inspect a specific tab or device, click on the **inspect** link on the respective option as shown in the following screenshot:

iOS debugging

On iOS devices, Safari has the capability of remote debugging with a feature of Safari web inspector. The steps required are as follows:

1. Open Safari on the iOS device.
2. It is required to connect your iOS device to the system.

3. Safari needs to be installed on the development machine too. Open the Safari browser.

4. Go to the **Develop** menu option on the top, and look for your device's name.

5. There will be a list of tabs open on your iOS device Safari browser that you can remote debug on your development machine.

Remote debugging using jsconsole.com

jsconsole is an online website that emulates the JavaScript command line tool. It enables you to bridge any remote WebView or browser and remotely receive logs and send JavaScript commands to the remote device. It is very useful for cases where you want to debug issues for remote users who cannot be with you.

The basic requirement is you have to inject a script tag generated online on jsconsole.com and put in the app or mobile web app that you want to debug. The steps that must be followed are:

1. Go to jsconsole.com.

2. Create a session using the command :listen on the website.

3. You will get a script tag with a unique URL that you have to copy and paste into index.html of your Ionic App.

4. Any calls to console.log from your Ionic App running on any remote device will now be logged onto the website jsconsole.com.

The following screenshot shows the output of the preceding steps:

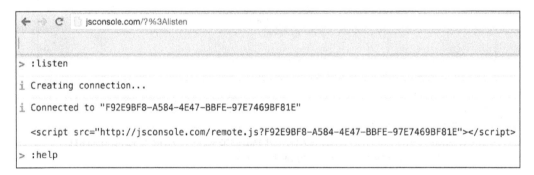

Testing using Ngrok

We have learned a lot about remote debugging but there is a problem such as hosting your Ionic App to a public location where any device on the Internet can access it. Also, sometimes you have to integrate your Ionic App to some local APIs and then test it on an actual device.

It would be very tedious and cumbersome to upload your backend and Ionic App to a public-facing server every time you want to test some functionality. Ngrok is an excellent tool that enables you to expose your local host server on any port to the Internet world using a public URL.

Ngrok acts as a secure tunnel between your local machine and a public URL, which people can access on any device. You can use this public URL in the methods given previously in this chapter to remotely debug your Ionic App.

Ngrok is very easy to use, you have to download it from the Internet. It will be downloaded as an archive, unzip it, and save it. You can also install using the `npm` command, `npm install -g ngrok`. Now open your Ionic App locally in the browser by using the command `ionic serve`.

Your app will open up in the browser on `http://localhost:<port_number>`. If we assume that the port number is `8100`, then you can start the Ngrok service by using the command `ngrok 8100` in the command line prompt [windows] or terminal [mac]. Ngrok will output a random public URL such as `s2323h4.ngrok.com`. You can use this URL to access your local Ionic App from any remote device and keep on testing or debugging. The following screenshot depicts the screen output when `ngrok` command is executed:

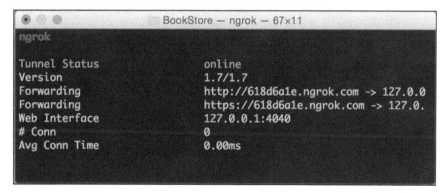

Summary

In this chapter we have learned different ways to test our Ionic App during development. We have also learnt different ways to share our app with co-collaborators or colleagues to get feedback. A Mobile App requires a lot of feedback from various users before publishing it to the public. In the next chapter we will learn how to integrate Cordova plugins into your Ionic App and leverage hardware features of your device such as camera, geolocation, and so on.

Working with Cordova Plugins – ngCordova

8

In the previous chapters we have learnt how to develop beautiful apps using Ionic components and integrate them into different backends. In this chapter we will learn how to leverage hardware features in Ionic Apps using Cordova plugins. A Mobile App has evolved today from more than just displaying or taking input for information. Mobile Apps have become more powerful in all walks of life, such as mediums for taking pictures from the camera, giving commands via voice, scanning barcodes of products, finding locations and services around us, biometric authorizations, and even helping us to keep fit. In a Hybrid App, utilizing the device capabilities is a bit tricky, but Cordova makes it easy.

ngCordova is an amazing open source library that has Angular wrappers around open source Cordova plugins. This library has a collection of services and extensions that were initially developed by the Ionic team but are driven by the community these days. In this chapter we will be covering the following topics:

- Introduction to Cordova plugins
- Integrating ngCordova to the Ionic App
- Important plugins
    - ° Camera plugin
    - ° Push notifications
    - ° Geolocation
    - ° Contacts
    - ° Network
    - ° Device sensors
- Custom Cordova plugin development

We will be learning about how to use the basic features of these plugins so that we can develop special features in our Ionic App using these.

We do not need to write any native code for any platform. The plugin includes the code for each native platform and also a JS file to expose the methods for consumption in JavaScript.

Introduction to Cordova plugins

Cordova's main purpose is to package web code into a Native App, but the second most important job is to create a bridge between the web(JS) code and the native code. Cordova ensures that Hybrid Apps harness the power and performance of native code perfectly. Cordova plugins utilize this power and enable us to use the specific device features in JS easily.

Cordova from version 3 and above decided to expose all device APIs as plugins. The Cordova plugin is a reusable set of code that contains the native code as well as JavaScript code. We know that our web app runs inside a WebView control in Ionic/Cordova Apps. The JavaScript code of the plugin exposes methods that will call a bridge/interface to invoke a native method for the respective platform such as iOS(Objective C) and Android(Java).

The contents of a Cordova plugin package are:

- Native code for each platform
- A common JavaScript library
- A manifest file called `plugin.xml`

The folder structure for the Cordova plugin project is:

```
// Main Plugin Folder
- plugin.xml
- src/
- android/
// Java (Android SDK) code
- ios/
// Objective-C code
- www/
// Javascript library
```

The Cordova library has the basic device API plugins developed, and can be integrated with your Ionic App easily. Cordova also maintains a list of third-party open source plugins available, which can be downloaded and added to your app too. If there is some functionality for which no plugins can be found, we will discuss the process for creating a custom plugin at high level.

Plugin management

In order to manage such a large list of in-house and third-party plugins, Cordova uses a plugin management system called Plugman. Plugman is a command line tool that enables features such as searching for a plugin, adding a new plugin, removing an existing plugin, or changing plugin configurations.

Integrating ngCordova to Ionic App

ngCordova is a JS library that acts as an Angular wrapper to all Cordova plugins. Angular has its own architectural style and hence Cordova plugins do not fit directly into an Ionic App. ngCordova makes it super easy for Ionic developers to call JS methods for Cordova plugins and process the data input.

ngCordova is available as a JS file, which can be added to your project using Bower if it is being used as a dependency management system. The `bower` command to install the specific ngCordova dependency into your Ionic App is as follows:

```
$ bower install ngCordova
```

The ngCordova JS file can also be directly downloaded from the GitHub website, `https://github.com/driftyco/ng-cordova/`. There will be two files in the `dist` folder, `ng-cordova.js` and `ng-cordova.min.js`. You can include the reference to one of these files in the `index.html` file of your Ionic App using the following code:

```
<script src="lib/ngCordova/dist/ng-cordova.min.js">
<script src="cordova.min.js">
```

The ngCordova JS file has a module named `ngCordova`, which contains services exposing functionalities for most of the popular Cordova plugins available online. We need to inject the ngCordova angular module into our Ionic App root module. We have to add the following code to `app.js`:

```
angular.module('myApp',['ngCordova']);
```

In order to use Cordova plugins in JavaScript, we need to wait for the `deviceready` event, which notifies us about the completion of loading of native code. The ngCordova plugin calls will not work before the device ready event is fired.

The Ionic platform provides an `Ionicready` event hook that is always executed after a device ready event. Any ngCordova code should be written inside this `$ionicPlatform.ready` event hook as follows:

```
// Named Callback Function
function executePluginCode() {
  $cordovaPlugin.someFunction().then(success, error);
}
$ionicPlatform.ready(executePluginCode);
```

Although ngCordova is used to invoke native code and handle responses, the actual heavy-weight work is being done by the Cordova plugins themselves. We have to manage the Cordova plugins from the Cordova command line tool or the Plugman tool separately. The list of Cordova plugins supported by ngCordova is given on its website. The code to add a new plugin is:

```
cordova plugin add <plugin_name>
```

 All the Cordova plugins do not work on browsers or emulators so please test your Ionic App on real devices using the methods mentioned in previous chapters for those plugins.

Important plugins

We will discuss a few important plugins that are required in most of the apps. These plugins are available for both iOS and Android, but we will discuss the common JS code here as the native code is abstracted from the developer.

Camera plugin

This plugin enables taking pictures and videos from the camera using your Ionic App and saving it to the local storage. This is available in the ngCordova module as the `$cordovaCamera` service. We have to use dependency injection to inject this service to any controller or service we want to use this in.

The command line to be executed using the Ionic/Cordova CLI is:

```
cordova plugin add cordova-plugin-camera
```

The `$cordovaCamera` service exposes one method `getPicture(options)` to invoke the native camera API. The object options passed to this method define the settings and the behavior of the action to be completed from the app. The options parameter is passed as an object containing the following optional properties/fields:

Options property name	Type	Description
quality	Number	Quality of the image, range of 0-100
cameraDirection	Number	Selection of camera—Back:0, Front-facing:1
sourceType	Number/ Enum	Setting the source for the picture, values supported: Camera. PictureSourceType. [PHOTOLIBRARY | CAMERA | SAVEDPHOTOALBUM]
mediaType	String	Choosing the type of media to select from
encodingType	Number	Type of image to save JPEG:0, PNG:1
correctOrientation	Boolean	Correct captured images in case of wrong orientation
destinationType	Number	Set the destination for the image, values supported: Camera.DestinationType. [FILE_URI | DATA_URL]
allowEdit	Boolean	Allow simple editing of image before selection
saveToPhotoAlbum	Boolean	Decide whether to save image to photo album on device
targetWidth	Number	Width to scale the image (pixels)
targetHeight	Number	Height to scale the image (pixels)

This method call returns the object with image data. It would contain the image data URL or the image file URL based on the options passed. In our BookStore sample app we can use this to click the photo of the book cover. The code to show the image using the data URL scheme is:

```
angular.module.controller('MyBookPictureCtrl', function($scope,
$cordovaCamera,$ionicPlatform) {
  $scope.bookImage = { src: '/img/dummyBookImage.jpg' };
  $scope.takeBookPhoto = function () {
    $ionicPlatform.ready(function () {
      var pluginOptions = {
        sourceType: Camera.PictureSourceType.CAMERA,
        encodingType: Camera.EncodingType.JPEG,
```

```
        saveToPhotoAlbum: false,
        destinationType: Camera.DestinationType.DATA_URL
      };
      $cordovaCamera.getPicture(pluginOptions).then(function(picData){
        $scope.bookImage = "data:image/jpeg;base64," + picData;
      }, function(err) {
        // error
      });
    });
  }
});
```

This is the code for saving the image to the local storage on the device. You will get the file location and data URL, which can be stored locally or on any remote server using web services:

```
angular.module.controller('MyBookPictureCtrl', function($scope,
$cordovaCamera,$ionicPlatform) {
  $scope.bookImage = { src: '/img/dummyBookImage.jpg' };
  $scope.takeBookPhoto = function () {
    $ionicPlatform.ready(function () {
      var pluginOptions = {
        sourceType: Camera.PictureSourceType.CAMERA,
        encodingType: Camera.EncodingType.PNG,
        destinationType: Camera.DestinationType.FILE_URI
      };
      $cordovaCamera.getPicture(pluginOptions).then(function(picURI) {
        $scope.bookImage = picURI;
      }, function(err) {
        // error
      });
    });
  }
});
```

In our BookStore App, we can add a feature to click a picture of a new book and store it for displaying in the book listing. The camera plugin can be used in a wide variety of use cases such as storing any scene, object state, saving memories, and so on.

Push Notifications

Mobile Apps need not poll the server for regular updates as they can leverage the push design pattern using Push Notifications technology. Implementing Push Notifications in Mobile Apps is tedious as it requires a middleware server integrating to cloud servers of all platforms such as the **Apple Push Notification Services (APNS)**, **Google Cloud Messaging (GCM)**, and the **Windows Push Notification Service (WNS)**.

We will not discuss the implementation of this middleware server. This server can be replaced by cloud push service providers such as Parse, Kinvey, and Ionic. Ionic push is very easy to configure and will work perfectly with the ngCordova push plugin. We will be discussing the ngCordova push plugin API to register, unregister, and receive Push Notifications. The command line to be executed using the Ionic/Cordova CLI is:

```
cordova plugin add https://github.com/phonegap-build/PushPlugin.git
```

After adding the plugin and ngCordova library, we can use the push plugin as the `$cordovaPush` service available in the ngCordova module. We have to inject this `$cordovaPush` service into any controller or service we want to use it.

In order to enable Push Notifications for a specific Mobile App on a device, the app needs to register its unique device ID. The method to register a device is:

- **Method Signature**: `register(config)`
    - **Returns**: Object (it will contain user info and device token (iOS) or `registrationId` (Android))
    - **Parameter**: The parameter `config` object to be passed can has the following fields:

Property name	Type	Platform	Description
badge	Boolean	iOS	Whether the Push Notification should have a badge.
sound	Boolean	iOS	Whether the Push Notification will have a sound alert.
alert	Boolean	IOS	Whether the Push Notification will show an alert.
senderID	String	Android	String representing a unique ID extracted from the Google cloud console specific to a project.

The second method to unregister a device has the following details:

- **Method Signature**: `unregister(options)`
  - ° **Returns**: Promise (it returns a promise that can be attached to a success handler or error handler)
  - ° **Parameters**: Options parameter to be passed is optional

The code example is as follows:

```
// Registering for Push Notifications
angular.module('BookStoreApp', ['ngCordova'])
.run(['$cordovaPush',function($cordovaPush) {
  var gcmConfig = {'sender_id':
    'sender_id_from_google_console'};
  $cordovaPush.register(gcmConfig).then(function(result) {
    // Result object will have a RegistrationId which you
    need to send to your middleware server
  }, function(err) {
    // Invoked if Error Received
  });
  $cordovaPush.unregister(gcmConfig).then(function(result)
  {
    // It will successfully unregister your device/app with GCM
  }, function(err) {
    // Invoked if Error Received
  });
});
```

The Push Notifications are received using angular events in the ngCordova library. The event name for the Push Notification is `$cordovaPush:notificationReceived`. The event can be listened using the `$on` method on `$rootScope`. The event will receive two arguments, event and notification object. The sample code for listening to Push Notifications and receiving them is as follows:

```
angular.module('BookStoreApp', ['ngCordova'])
.run(['$cordovaPush','$rootScope',function($cordovaPush,$rootScope)
{
  $rootScope.$on('$cordovaPush:notificationReceived',
  function(event, pushNotif) {
    if (pushNotif.alert) {
      navigator.notification.alert(pushNotif.alert);
    }
    if (pushNotif.sound) {
      var alert = new Media(event.sound);
      alert.play();
```

```
    }
    // notification.title & notification.message will be the main
    fields
  });
});
```

Push Notifications can also have custom payload, depending on the server sending it. We can process the Push Notification and implement custom logic on receiving the push.

Geolocation

The Geolocation Cordova plugin is used to get the current location of your device. It can also get continuous location of your device tracking the movement of the device. The service $cordovaGeolocation available in the module ngCordova can be used to integrate the Geolocation plugin to your Ionic App.

The command line to be executed using the Ionic/Cordova CLI is:

```
cordova plugin add cordova-plugin-geolocation
```

The methods available in this service are given as follows:

- **Method Name**: getCurrentPosition(options)
    - **Returns**: Promise (the success handler of promise receives a position object containing coordinates including latitude, longitude, altitude, speed, and so on)
    - **Parameter**: The options parameter can have three fields: timeout (number) — the number of milliseconds to wait for a response, maximumAge (number) — the number of milliseconds defining the age of the cached response that will be accepted, and enableHighAccuracy (Boolean) — guiding the plugin to provide the best results

The code example is as follows:

```
$scope.findBooksNearby = function() {
  var configOpts = {timeout: 2500, enableHighAccuracy:
    true};
  $cordovaGeolocation
  .getCurrentPosition(configOpts)
  .then(function (pos) {
    var lat  = pos.coords.latitude;
    var long = pos.coords.longitude;
    // Pass lat & long to your service for finding books
    nearby
```

```
  }, function(errorObj) {
    // Invoked if Error Received
  });
}
```

- **Method Name**: watchPosition(options)
  - ○ **Returns**: watchId Promise (every time the position changes, the success handler of promise receives a position object containing coordinates including latitude, longitude, altitude, speed, and so on.)

    The watchId object returned will be used in the next method to stop watching position changes.

  - ○ **Parameter**: The options parameter can have three fields: timeout (number) – the number of milliseconds to wait for a response, maximumAge (number) – the number of milliseconds defining the age of the cached response that will be accepted, and enableHighAccuracy (boolean) – guiding the plugin to provide the best results.

- **Method Name**: clearWatch(watchID)
  - ○ **Returns**: Promise (standard promise registering success or error callback).
  - ○ **Parameter**: watchID returned from the watchPosition method.

The code example is as follows:

```
$scope.movementCoords = [];
var watchMovement;
$scope.trackMovement = function(){watchMovement =
$cordovaGeolocation.watchPosition(configOpts);
  watch.then(null,
  function(err) { // error },
  function(positionCoords) { // position object
    $scope.movementCoords.push(positionCoords);
  });
}
$scope.clearTracking = function () {
  $cordovaGeolocation.clearWatch(watchMovement)
  .then(function(result) { // Success in stop recording
  movement },
    function (error) {  // Error invoked if unable to stop});
}
```

Contacts

A contacts plugin is used to manage the contacts on the device. It is available for both iOS and Android. It has two major methods—one for saving a new contact and the other for fetching contacts based on some parameters. The service `$cordovaContacts` is available under the ngCordova module for managing the contacts plugin.

The command line to be executed using the Ionic/Cordova CLI is:

```
cordova plugin add cordova-plugin-contacts
```

The methods available under this service are:

- **Method Name**: save (contact)
    - ○ **Returns**: Promise (standard promise registering success or error callback)
    - ○ **Parameter**: The Contact object should be passed as a parameter, the contact object can have these common properties: displayName (string), name (string), phoneNumbers (array), emails (array), and birthday (date)

- **Method Name**: find (filterOptions)
    - ○ **Returns**: Promise (standard promise registering success or error callback)—the success callback returns the list of contacts fetched
    - ○ **Parameter**: The filterOptions object, which can contain the properties—filter (string[searchTerm]), multiple (boolean), fields (array[to be searched]), and desiredFileds (array[returned fields])

The code example is as follows:

```
$scope.addNewFriend = function(userInfo) {
  // Saving New Contact from userInfo object
  $cordovaContacts.save(userInfo).then(function(result) {
    // New Contact is written to device.
  }, function(err) {
    // Error invoked if unsuccessful.
  });
}

$scope.findFriends = function() {
  var opts = { filter : 'searchTerm',
    multiple: true,
    fields: [ 'displayName', 'name' ]
    desiredFields: ['id','name']
```

```
    };
    $cordovaContacts.find(opts).then(function(filteredContacts)
    {
      $scope.friendsSearchResult = filteredContacts;
    });
}
```

Network

The network device plugin helps in identifying the network on which the device is connected and listening to network change events. The $cordovaNetwork is a service of the ngCordova module, which exposes multiple methods and events for managing the network.

The command line to be executed using the Ionic/Cordova CLI is:

cordova plugin add cordova-plugin-network-information

The methods available under this service are:

- **Method Name**: getNetwork()
  - ○ **Returns**: The Connection object (this property determines the connection state and connection type)

The possible connection types can be:

Type	Description
Connection.UNKNOWN	Unknown connection
Connection.ETHERNET	Ethernet connection
Connection.WIFI	Wi-Fi connection
Connection.CELL_2G	Cell 2G connection
Connection.CELL_2G	Cell 3G connection
Connection.CELL_2G	Cell 4G connection
Connection.CELL	Cell generic connection
Connection.NONE	No network connection

- **Method Name**: isOnline()
  - ◦ **Returns**: Boolean (true if network is online)

- **Method Name**: isOffline()
  - ◦ **Returns**: Boolean (true if network is offline)

There are two events that this service exposes, which help us in listening to changes in the network such as notifying when the device goes online or offline

- **Event Name**: $cordovaNetwork (online) — this is fired when the device goes online
  - ◦ **Returns**: Event (Angular Event Object), Network State (Network state/type of the connection)

- **Event Name**: $cordovaNetwork (offline) — this is fired when the device goes offline
  - ◦ **Returns**: Event (Angular Event Object), Network State (Network state/type of the connection)

The code example is as follows:

```
angular.module('BookStoreApp',['ngCordova'])
.run(['$cordovaNetwork','$rootScope',function($cordovaNetwo
rk, $rootScope) { $rootScope.networkType =
  $cordovaNetwork.getNetwork(); $rootScope.isDeviceOnline =
  $cordovaNetwork.isOnline(); $rootScope.isDeviceOffline =
  $cordovaNetwork.isOffline();
  // Handling online event & updating $rootScope flag
  $rootScope.$on('$cordovaNetwork:online', function(event,
  networkState){
    $rootScope.networkType = networkState.type;
    $rootScope.isDeviceOnline = true;
  });
  // Handling offline event & updating $rootScope flag
  $rootScope.$on('$cordovaNetwork:offline', function(event,
  networkState){
    $rootScope.networkType = networkState.type;
    $rootScope.isDeviceOffline = true;
  });
});
```

Device sensors

The mobile device has a lot of sensors such as accelerometer, gyrosensor, and compass, which are being used by a variety of Mobile Apps in the health, transportation, gaming, and so on, sectors. We can leverage these device sensor inputs in our Ionic App using device services in the ngCordova module.

Device motion

The device motion is managed using the `$cordovaDeviceMotion` service of the ngCordova module. This plugin provides access to the device accelerometer. It reports the change in speed or movement of the device in three dimensions (x, y, and z).

The command line to be executed using the Ionic/Cordova CLI is:

```
cordova plugin add cordova-plugin-device-motion
```

The methods available under this service are:

- **Method Name**: `getAcceleration()`
    - **Description**: It fetches the current acceleration along the x, y, and z axes
    - **Returns**: Object (contains the x, y, z coordinates and timestamp)

- **Method Name**: watchAcceleration(options)
    - **Description**: It fetches the device's current acceleration at regular intervals
    - **Returns**: Promise WatchID (success handler object contains the x, y, z coordinates and timestamp)
    - **Parameters**: Options (the options object should have a frequency property whose value should be in milliseconds defining the interval after which a new acceleration will be fetched)

- **Method Name**: `clearWatch (watchID)`
    - **Description**: It clears the watchAcceleration regular calls
    - **Parameters**: `watchID` (the id returned by watchAcceleration() call)

The code example is as follows:

```
$scope.accelerationData = [];
var watchId =
$cordovaDeviceMotion.watchAcceleration(configOpts);
watchId.then(null,
  function(error) {
    // An error occurred
  },
  function(response) {
    $scope.accelerationData.push({
      x:response.x,
      y:response.y,z:response.z, timestamp:response.timestamp
    })
  ;});
$cordovaDeviceMotion.clearWatch(watchId)
.then(function(result) {
  // Stopped listening to motion changes
}, function (error) {
// Error in stopping the event listener
});
```

Device orientation

The device orientation is managed using the $cordovaDeviceOrientation service of the ngCordova module. This plugin provides access to the device compass sensor. It helps in identifying the direction or heading that the device is pointed to. It measures the heading in degrees from 0 to 355.9, where 0 is north.

The command line to be executed using the Ionic/Cordova CLI is:

```
cordova plugin add org.apache.cordova.device-orientation
```

The methods available under this service are:

* **Method Name**: getCurrentHeading()
    ◦ **Description**: It fetches the current compass heading reading
    ◦ **Returns**: Object (contains magneticHeading, trueHeading, headingAccuracy, and timestamp)

- **Method Name**: watchHeading(options)
  - ° **Description**: It fetches the device's current heading at regular intervals
  - ° **Returns**: Promise WatchID (success handler object contains magneticHeading, trueHeading, headingAccuracy, and timestamp)
  - ° **Parameters**: Options (the options object should have a frequency property whose value should be in milliseconds defining the interval after which a new acceleration will be fetched)

- **Method Name**: clearWatch(watchID)
  - ° **Description**: It clears the watchHeading regular calls
  - ° **Parameters**: watchID (the id returned by watchHeading() call)

The code example is as follows:

```
$scope.headingData = [];
var watchId =
$cordovaDeviceOrientation.watchHeading(configOpts);
watchId.then(null, function(error)
{
  // An error occurred
},
function(response) {
  $scope.headingData.push({
    magneticHeading:response.magneticHeading,
    trueHeading:response.trueHeading,
    accuracy:response.headingAccuracy,
    timeStamp:response.timestamp
  });
});
$cordovaDeviceOrientation.clearWatch(watchId)
.then(function(result) {
  // Stopped listening to compass changes
}, function (error) {
  // Error in stopping the event listener
});
```

Custom Cordova plugin development

There are multiple third-party open source plugins available that can be integrated to your Ionic App along with the ngCordova library. If we do not find the required functionality plugin, we can develop a custom Cordova plugin and use it along with the ngCordova library.

We have to write the native code for each platform we want to port our plugin on. The native coding part will be standard according to the procedures followed in the respective native platform. Cordova helps in exposing the same functionality using the native hybrid bridge. In your JavaScript file, you should call the following method to invoke the native functionality:

```
cordova.exec(successCallback, failureCallback, service, action,
[args]);
```

The previous code will execute/invoke the action method on the service class on the native side. If the native code completes successfully, it will call the successCallback or, if it fails, it will call failureCallback. The detailed process to develop a custom plugin is beyond the scope of this book.

Summary

In this chapter we have learned how custom Cordova plugins help in integrating the native device features in a Hybrid App. We have also learnt how to use the ngCordova library in our Ionic App to integrate the device plugins and use them in our controllers and views. We have also seen the utility of the most important device plugins and API services available under the ngCordova library.

9
Future of Ionic

Ionic has evolved from a framework to an ecosystem. Ionic started initially as a JS framework for developing a Hybrid Mobile App front end but it has come a long way and there is more to come. Ionic has become a platform to empower next gen Mobile Apps through web technologies and cloud services. In this chapter we will learn about these cloud services, which you can use to empower or augment the Ionic Apps you have built using this book. Also, we will discuss the future of the Ionic JS framework into its version 2, which will be based on Angular 2 involving a re-haul of the architecture using new technologies such as ES6/2015.

Ionic has launched the initial alpha version of v2 and it will take some time for it to stabilize. We will discuss the new features and migration strategy for v2. Ionic also has launched a portal, `ionic.io,` for managing all the cloud services it provides. We will discuss an overview of all these services. In this chapter we will discuss the following topics:

- Ionic cloud services
    - Ionic Creator
    - Ionic Market
    - Ionic Push
    - Ionic Deploy
    - Ionic Analytics
    - Ionic Package
    - Ionic Lab

- Ionic v2
    - New features
    - Migrating to v2

These cloud services are available to developers for free in alpha version, so we should try all of them in order to learn about their true benefit. Also, Ionic v2 is the next succession path for Ionic v1 apps developed, so we should know what's new and also devise a migration path for the same.

Ionic cloud services

Mobile Apps have evolved from simple games or calculator apps to become more like communities and platforms for social engagement. All popular Mobile Apps must have features such as social sharing, collaboration, and Push Notifications these days. These features, if developed for each Mobile App, can account for a lot of effort. Ionic has launched this cloud platform `ionic.io`, which provides cloud services to be integrated into existing Ionic Apps using SDKs for each platform. A signup is required for using all these products and services on `ionic.io`.

Ionic Creator

Ionic Creator is an online GUI wizard to create Ionic Apps using a drag and drop utility. We have already discussed Ionic Creator in detail in *Chapter 3, Start Building Your First Ionic App*. Ionic Creator can also be used to design a few of the views for your app.

Ionic Creator can manage multiple views and also manage the links between different views. It provides an easy-to-use interface to drag and drop components or UI elements from the side panel. Almost all types of components or elements are available such as button, image, button bar, popups, and even custom HTML. The code for the views designed using Ionic creator can be exported and downloaded as a ZIP file. It will hold HTML, CSS, and JavaScript files, which can be integrated with your existing Ionic App too.

Ionic Market

Ionic has set to change the industry with a robust Hybrid App development framework. Ionic has been instrumental in creating a strong community of developers creating amazing Ionic Apps and components. Ionic Market is a platform to empower this growing community of Ionic developers. Here is a screenshot for the Ionic Market web page:

Ionic Market is available for developers to showcase their code and distribute it either for free or for a fee. Ionic Library involves the basic components and features that can be used to develop Mobile Apps. Generally, developers require much more complex reusable components and features to develop their apps rapidly. It is very hard to find awesome work done by other developers by searching online through their distributed codebases.

Ionic Market enables developers to upload and submit listings for their starter templates, Ionic plugins (Ionic re-usable code), themes (Scss/CSS files). Anyone with an `ionic.io` platform can buy or sell starters, plugins, or themes on this open exchange platform. Developers can also link their listings to any third-party marketplace where they would be selling their components primarily.

Ionic Market does not even charge anything or take any cut, except the payment platform charges or any taxes involved in the buying/selling of these digital pieces. I would recommend you to list your Ionic Apps/components if you want to earn while being an awesome Ionic developer.

Ionic Push

Push Notifications are always tricky to implement for any Mobile App. Apart from using the push plugin in a Hybrid App, we also require a backend that can send Push Notifications to cloud servers of multiple platforms such as iOS, Android, and Windows. Ionic Push saves a lot of development effort and helps developers get to the market faster without any investment in a backend.

Ionic Push integrates very well with the push plugin and the ngCordova library. Simple configurations are required to make it work and Ionic push provides an easy-to-use console to manage the sending of Push Notifications. We will describe the basic steps to enable `ionic.io` and Ionic push to be used with your Ionic App:

- **Step 1**: In order to use the `ionic.io` SDK in our app, we need to add a web-client component using the Ionic CLI tool only. We should also add the push plugin at the same time using the following code:

```
ionic plugin add phonegap-plugin-push
ionic add ionic-platform-web-client
```

- **Step 2**: Ionic CLI also provides commands for managing the Ionic io modules. We have to initialize `ionic.io` for our app. We can run the following command from the root folder of our Ionic App:

```
ionic io init
```

- **Step 3**: You can now use the Ionic push angular services to write code to register a device for Push Notifications and also listen to events for receiving Push Notifications. The `ionic.service.core` and `ionic.service.push` modules are required to be injected for this.

- **Step 4**: Now, we need to configure our app to receive Push Notifications. This needs a special setup and configurations for iOS and Android. iOS Push Notifications are mediated by **APNS (Apple Push Notification Services)** and Android by **GCM (Google Cloud Messaging)**. The detailed guide for setting up is available at the links http://docs.ionic.io/docs/push-ios-setup (iOS) and http://docs.ionic.io/docs/push-android-setup (Android).

  We can also test Push Notifications using Ionic push without even doing these configurations for all the platforms using the dev mode. These are fake notifications generated by the `ionic.io` module.

- **Step 5**: Integrating your backend for listening to push registrations and sending Push Notifications. There are two ways in which you can perform these actions. You can either use the `ionic.io` cloud console to see the devices registered and even send Push Notifications using a simple interface, or you can use their REST API to call these methods from your own backend server and listen to push registrations and send Push Notifications.

  You can register your backend webhook URL to receive the push registration events using the following command:

```
ionic push webhook_url http://your-server-url
```

It will be hit with a HTTP POST request with the device token and extra keys to identify the user every time a new device is registered using Ionic Push.

The REST API endpoint to send a push is `https://push.ionic.io/api/v1/push` [HTTP POST]. The details about headers and payload to be passed to this request can be found at the URL `https://push.ionic.io/api/v1/push`. Ionic push enables you to send an instant Push Notification or even schedule one for later delivery to all users or specific user IDs. Here is a screenshot for the dashboard for composing a Push Notification:

Ionic Deploy

Once your apps are on the public app stores such as the Apple app store and Google Play store, the update cycles are pretty lengthy. It is a tedious job to submit a new update to the app store and go through the complete review process. It takes at least a few days or even weeks for your updated app to be released online. Your users also have to go to the respective app store and download the complete updated version of the app.

Ionic Deploy (in alpha state) solves this problem by giving the capability to the developers for updating their apps on the fly. It enables on-demand improvements and enhancements done on the app to reach the users immediately. It does not require recompilation and updating the build anywhere. It also supports rollback to a previous version instantly. Ionic deploy can also be used for collaborating with designers and testers during the development of the app.

Using Ionic Deploy

In order to leverage the benefits of Ionic Deploy, you can upload your Ionic App to cloud servers using the `ionic upload` command. This would upload your web assets of the Ionic App to a cloud server. The uploaded content will always be augmented with a unique version number and a timestamp. Ionic deploy also lets you create separate builds for separate people using something called Deploy Channels. Any update can be sent to a specific Deploy Channel and will be sent to the apps installed with that specific deploy channel. Default channels named `production`, `stage`, and `dev` already exist and can be used immediately. Alternatively, the developer can decide to create any custom deploy channel also. For more details on Ionic deploy please go to the URL `http://docs.ionic.io/docs/deploy-overview`. The following screenshot will appear:

Ionic Deploy

Here you can create and manage deploys, allowing you to push updates out to users of your app in realtime.

Ionic Analytics

Ionic Analytics is the latest alpha state cloud service launched under the `ionic.io` platform, which enables users to track important metrics and usage data for their app users. It is very important for developers to know about important insights into the usage of their app so that they can plan for enhancements or updates. Data and facts are always essential for making the right decisions and this service from Ionic helps you take wise decisions for your Ionic Apps. Existing analytics platforms do not have a lot of tools for Hybrid Mobile Apps.

Ionic Analytics takes care of everything for Hybrid Mobile App needs and requires no other analytics suite to coexist. Ionic Analytics fits right in because it knows the internal architecture and working of an Ionic App including routing, controllers, and components. Ionic Analytics uses events to record data from user interactions. The event consists of an event name and the associated data for it.

The `$ionicAnalytics` service of the `ionic.service.analytics` module is used to send event data automatically as soon as the user interacts with your app. There are a lot of built-in events that are automatically sent but are configurable using the `$ionicAutoTrackProvider`. The `$ionicAnalytics` service also enables developers to register custom events and send custom data for these events in your Ionic App code using the `track(name,dataObject)` method. Here is a screenshot for the dashboard to view the events:

Ionic Package

We have already learned in previous chapters how difficult it is to set up development environments for different iOS and Android platforms and then package the app. In order to save developer's efforts from these hassles, the Ionic Package cloud service has been released under `ionic.io`. It is a cloud service that automatically packages the app on the go and provides ready to release packages for iOS and Android platforms. This cloud service does not even require a Mac machine for iOS builds, but the Apple Developer license needs to be procured as mentioned in one of the previous chapters.

Ionic package enables developers to build dev or production packages using simple commands under the ionic CLI command set. These packages can be submitted to a public app store or directly installed on a friend/collaborator's device. The sample command to make a build for a specific platform is:

```
ionic package build android --profile PROFILE_TAG
```

Details regarding more Ionic Package options can be found at `http://docs.ionic.io/docs/package-overview`.

Ionic Lab

We have seen that there are a lot of commands and configurations for developers to remember. In this era of automation and self service, Ionic has come up with a beautiful GUI tool called Ionic Lab for Mac and Windows to help developers create Ionic Apps easily. It includes all the features to manage your Ionic Apps on a development machine end to end. In my opinion it is a life savior for people who do not like terminal but love user experience.

Ionic Lab provides a user-friendly way to perform all the operations we have seen Ionic CLI commands for in this book. It also provides a live preview for your app for testing it. The overview of capabilities for Ionic Lab are:

- **App creation**: You can create a new app with a click of a button using any of the starters available
- **Running app**: You can run any app on a simulator or device from the Ionic Lab GUI
- **Make builds**: You can click a button to generate a build for any platform
- **Preview app**: Ionic Lab has a live preview feature for testing your app
- **Upload app**: An easy button to upload the app to the `ionic.io` server for it to be viewed on devices using Ionic view is also provided
- **App logs**: An interface to view the logs for your Ionic App is also provided

Ionic v2

The Ionic team has recently announced the alpha version of Ionic 2 at an Angular Connect conference in London in October 2015. The Ionic team has worked closely with the Angular 2 team to align the Ionic 2 perfectly with the Angular 2 release. This has also given the opportunity to improve the base architecture of Ionic and move towards more performant Hybrid Mobile Apps. Ionic 2 has an improved routing and navigation methodology and also an optimized way of integrating with native APIs.

New features

We will be discussing the new features in Ionic v2 briefly in this section.

Angular 2, ES6, and Typescript

As Angular 2 has decided to leverage ES6/ES2015, the latest version of JavaScript that supports classes and other exciting features, Ionic 2 apps will also be written with ES6 or Typescript. Typescript is an extended version of ES6 with the support for types. We can leverage classes, ES6 modules, decorators, arrow functions, and block scopes.

Abstracted annotations

Although Ionic 2 is built on top of Angular 2, the Ionic team has baked in a nice abstractions that would help you overcome the fear of Angular 2. For example, the new annotation @App built by the Ionic team over the existing Angular 2 annotations. It will be super easy for any developer who knows just the basics of Angular 2 to make apps using Ionic 2.

Material design

Ionic has developed special theming for the Android platform to support the popular material design conceptualized by Google.

Enhanced Native Integration

Ionic 2 boasts about direct integration of more native APIs into the platform so that no external plugins are required to build Mobile Apps. It would make it easy for Ionic Apps to harness the power of the device they are running on.

Powerful Theming

Ionic v1 lacked an important feature such as theming. Ionic v2 solves that problem and improves the theming apart from the basic platform-specific themes. Ionic v2 makes it easy to customize themes according to your own brand guidelines or color preferences. The theming will be managed by SASS stylesheets only.

Improved navigation and routing

Ionic has re-engineered the routing and navigation pieces in v2 to make it more app-like. The navigation enables you to link to even any sub view-like modal of a view, component, and so on. It will bring a more app-like experience to the users and enable deep linking in your Ionic v2 Apps.

Migration to v2

Ionic v1 will be supported by the Ionic team for a long time and we will not need to convert all our production apps to v2. The Ionic team will release enhancements and new features for Ionic v1 to make the migration path to v2 much easier.

A few important points regarding migration:

- Learning the basics of Angular 2 are very important for migrating your apps
- Learning all the new cool constructs in ES6 will also help in the ease of migration
- All the components and plugins from v1 are still there in v2 with the underlying concepts; most of them have not changed
- The views and controllers from v1 have been merged into one using @Page annotation and ES6 classes
- There are new entities called components that can be navigated to directly
- In your Ionic v1 apps, try to use the controller as syntax to make the migration very easy at a later stage
- Convert your code into ES6 or Typescript as valid JavaScript is valid Typescript, so that your app will not break even if you change only a small part

Summary

We have learned about the new cloud offerings from Ionic as a complete platform and how we can leverage them to make Ionic Apps rapidly and release them onto the market. We have also learned about the uber cool features of Ionic v2 and how we can plan to migrate our apps in the future.

Web developers now can develop fully featured Hybrid Mobile Apps using Ionic. In this book, we have learned how to use different components and services to add amazing user experience to our Ionic Apps. We can also leverage the native device features to enhance our Ionic Apps. We should also empower our Mobile Apps with mBaaS for providing a strong backend. The next step for Ionic developers should be to design and develop new components and share them with the online Ionic community.

Index

Symbols

$http constructor method 85, 86
$http services
  $http constructor method 85, 86
  about 84, 85
  response object 85
$ionicConfigProvider 81
$ionicGesture service
  about 74
  off method 75
  on method 74
$ionicLoading service 78
$ionicModal service
  about 79
  IonicModal controller 79

A

anatomy, Hybrid Mobile Application
  about 4
  custom WebView 5
  native code, calling to JS Bridge 6
  native library 5
AngularJS
  about 6
  concepts 7
  controllers 8
  directive 8
  expressions 11
  filters 11
  modules 7
  services 9, 10
  templates 10

Angular UI Router
  about 46
  abstract state 49
  dot notation, using 47
  multiple views, setting 49
  nested states 47
  object-based states, using 48
  parent property, using 48
  state parameters 50
  states 46, 47
  transition, to state 48
  URLs 46, 47
  views 47
Apache Cordova
  using 11
Apple Push Notification Service
  (APNS) 115, 130

B

blank template 38
BooksFactory 88, 89
BookStore
  about 42
  architecture 42
  design 42
  features 42
  layout 59
  navigation 59
buttons, CSS components
  about 63, 64
  bar 64
  icon buttons 64

C

camera plugin 112-114
capabilities, Ionic Lab
  app creation 134
  app logs 134
  app, previewing 134
  app, running 134
  builds, making 134
CDN-hosted library files
  using 28, 29
Code Editors
  about 25
  brackets 25
  Sublime Text 26
  Visual Studio 26
config method 7
contacts plugin 119
controllers, AngularJS 8, 9
Cordova plugin
  about 110
  custom development 125
  managing 111
cross compiled Hybrid Apps 3
CSS components
  about 62
  buttons 63
  cards 66
  footer 63
  forms 67
  grid 70
  header 62
  input elements 67
  lists 65
  tabs 69
  utility 71

D

Dependency Injection (DI) 7, 86
directives
  <ion-content> directive 37
  <ion-footer-bar> directive 55
  <ion-header-bar> directive 54
  <ion-nav-bar> directive 59
  <ion-nav-title> directive 59
  <ion-side-menu-content> directive 58
  <ion-side-menu> directive 57
  <ion-side-menus> directive 57
  <ion-tab> directive 56, 57
  <ion-tabs> directive 55, 56
  <ion-view> directive 59
dummy app
  building 23, 24

E

expressions, AngularJS 11

F

features, Ionic v2
  abstracted annotations 135
  Angular 2 134
  enhanced native integration 135
  ES6 134
  improved navigation and routing 135
  material design 135
  powerful theming 135
  Typescript 134
files, Ionic Project
  bower.json 34
  config.xml 34
  gulpfile.js 34
  package.json 34
filters, AngularJS 11
Firebase
  integration 95
  URL 95
folders, Ionic Project
  hooks 34
  platforms 34
  plugins 34
  resources 34
  scss 35
  www 35
form inputs, JS components
  <ion-checkbox> directive 73
  <ion-radio> directive 74
  <ion-toggle> directive 74
  about 73

G

Geolocation Cordova plugin 117, 118
gesture events
  about 75
  on-double-tap 75
  on-drag 75
  on-drag-down 76
  on-drag-left 76
  on-drag-right 76
  on-drag-up 75
  on-hold 75
  on-release 75
  on-swipe 76
  on-swipe-down 76
  on-swipe-left 76
  on-swipe-right 76
  on-swipe-up 76
  on-tap 75
  on-touch 75
Google Cloud Messaging (GCM) 115, 130
grid, CSS components 70

H

Hybrid Mobile Application
  about 1, 2
  anatomy 4
  types 3

I

input elements, CSS components
  about 67
  checkbox 68
  radio button list 68
  range control 69
  toggle control 69
Ionic Analytics 132
Ionic App
  ngCordova, integrating to 111, 112
Ionic cloud services
  about 128
  Ionic Analytics 132
  Ionic Creator 128
  Ionic Deploy 131

Ionic Lab 133
Ionic Market 128, 129
Ionic Package 133
Ionic Push 129-131
Ionic Creator
  about 28, 128
  used, for designing Ionic Project 30-32
  used, for designing prototype 30
Ionic Deploy
  about 131
  URL 132
  using 132
Ionic Factory 88
Ionic Framework
  about 12
  back menus 59
  navigation support 59
  using, with Brackets 25
  using, with different Code Editors 25
  using, with Visual Studio 26
Ionic header and footer
  <ion-footer-bar> directive 54
  <ion-header-bar> directive 54
  about 53
Ionic Lab
  about 32, 133
  capabilities 134
Ionic Market 128, 129
IonicModal controller
  about 79
  initialize(options) 79
Ionic Package
  about 133
  URL 133
Ionic Play
  about 25
  URL 25
Ionic Project
  <ion-content> directive 37
  <ion-pane> directive 37, 38
  anatomy 33
  app.js 36
  building 28
  components 35
  folders and files 33

folder structure 33
index.html file 35
root module 36
Ionic Project, building
CDN-hosted library files, using 28, 29
Ionic CLI, using locally 32
Ionic Creator, using for prototype
design 30, 31
Ionic Push
about 129
enabling 130, 131
Ionic services
authentication service 86, 87
versus factories 86
Ionic side menu
<ion-side-menu-content> directive 58
<ion-side-menu> directive 57, 58
<ion-side-menus> directive 57
<menu-close> directive 58
about 57
expose-aside-when 58
menu-toggle 58
Ionic starter template
about 38
blank template 38
maps template 41
sidemenu template 40, 41
tabs template 38, 39
Ionic Tabs
<ion-tab> directive 56, 57
<ion-tabs> directive 55, 56
about 55
Ionic v2
about 134
migrating to 136
new features 134
iOS Push Notifications
URL 130
issues
about 24
Git command-line tool not installed 24
npm global modules 24
permission issue [Mac or Linux] 24

J

JS components
$ionicActionSheet 72
$ionicBackdrop 73
$ionicGesture service 74
$ionicLoading 78
$ionicModal 79
$ionicPopover 80
about 71
events 74
form inputs 73
gesture events 75
gestures 74
ion-spinner 80
lists 76

L

lists, CSS components
about 65
buttons 66
dividers 65
icons 65
item avatars 66
thumbnails 66
lists, JS components
<ion-list> directive 76
about 76

M

maps template 41
mBaaS
Anypresence 91
Azure Mobile Services 91
demystifying 91
Firebase 91
Kinvey 91
Parse 91
miscellaneous components
$ionicConfigProvider 81
$ionicPosition 80

Mobile Apps
about 83
developing, with web technologies 6
multiple views 49

N

named view
about 49
relative, versus abstract 50
network device plugin
about 120, 121
sensors 122
ngCordova
integrating, to Ionic App 111, 112
URL 111

O

options property
allowEdit 113
cameraDirection 113
correctOrientation 113
destinationType 113
encodingType 113
mediaType 113
quality 113
saveToPhotoAlbum 113
sourceType 113
targetHeight 113
targetWidth 113

P

Parse
Analytics 92
API keys, obtaining 93
app, creating 92
Core 92
integrating, REST API used 93
integrating, SDK used 93
integration 92
platform sections 92
Push 92
setting configuration 93
URL 92

plugins
about 112
camera plugin 112-114
contacts plugin 119
Geolocation Cordova plugin 117, 118
push notifications 115, 116

Q

query parameters
$stateParams service 52
about 51
multiple parameters 52
single parameter 51

R

resolve property 53
response object
config property 85
data property 85
headers property 85
status property 85
statusText property 85
REST API
and $resource 90
used, for Parse integration 93
using 94

S

SDK
downloading 93
overview 93
used, for Parse integration 93
sensors, network device plugin
device motion 122
orientation 123
services, AngularJS 9, 10
show method options
buttonClicked 72
buttons 72
cancel 72
cancelOnStateChange 72
cancelText 72
cssClass 72

  destructiveButtonClicked 72
  destructiveText 72
  titleText 72
sidemenu template 40, 41
single page architecture (SPA) 6
state events
  $stateChangeError 53
  $stateChangeStart 52
  $stateChangeSuccess 52
  $stateNotFound 52
  about 52
state parameters
  about 50
  basic parameters 51
  query parameters 51
  Regex parameters 51
Sublime Text
  about 26
  URL 26

T

tabs, CSS components 69
templates, AngularJS 10
types, Hybrid Mobile Application
  cross compiled 3
  WebView-based 3

U

utility classes, CSS components 71

W

web technologies
  used, for developing Mobile Apps 6
WebView-based Hybrid Apps 3
Windows Push Notification Service
  (WNS) 115

Thank you for buying
Getting Started with Ionic

About Packt Publishing

Packt, pronounced 'packed', published its first book, *Mastering phpMyAdmin for Effective MySQL Management*, in April 2004, and subsequently continued to specialize in publishing highly focused books on specific technologies and solutions.

Our books and publications share the experiences of your fellow IT professionals in adapting and customizing today's systems, applications, and frameworks. Our solution-based books give you the knowledge and power to customize the software and technologies you're using to get the job done. Packt books are more specific and less general than the IT books you have seen in the past. Our unique business model allows us to bring you more focused information, giving you more of what you need to know, and less of what you don't.

Packt is a modern yet unique publishing company that focuses on producing quality, cutting-edge books for communities of developers, administrators, and newbies alike. For more information, please visit our website at www.packtpub.com.

About Packt Open Source

In 2010, Packt launched two new brands, Packt Open Source and Packt Enterprise, in order to continue its focus on specialization. This book is part of the Packt Open Source brand, home to books published on software built around open source licenses, and offering information to anybody from advanced developers to budding web designers. The Open Source brand also runs Packt's Open Source Royalty Scheme, by which Packt gives a royalty to each open source project about whose software a book is sold.

Writing for Packt

We welcome all inquiries from people who are interested in authoring. Book proposals should be sent to author@packtpub.com. If your book idea is still at an early stage and you would like to discuss it first before writing a formal book proposal, then please contact us; one of our commissioning editors will get in touch with you.

We're not just looking for published authors; if you have strong technical skills but no writing experience, our experienced editors can help you develop a writing career, or simply get some additional reward for your expertise.

Learning Ionic

ISBN: 978-1-78355-260-3   Paperback: 388 pages

Build real-time and hybrid mobile applications
with Ionic

1. Create hybrid mobile applications by
   combining the capabilities of Ionic,
   Cordova, and AngularJS.

2. Reduce the time to market your application
   using Ionic, that helps in rapid application
   development.

3. Detailed code examples and explanations,
   helping you get up and running with Ionic
   quickly and easily.

PhoneGap Mobile Application Development Cookbook

ISBN: 978-1-84951-858-1   Paperback: 320 pages

Over 40 recipes to create mobile applications
using the PhoneGap API with examples and
clear instructions

1. Use the PhoneGap API to create native mobile
   applications that work on a wide range of
   mobile devices.

2. Discover the native device features and
   functions you can access and include within
   your applications.

3. Packed with clear and concise examples to
   show you how to easily build native mobile
   applications.

Please check **www.PacktPub.com** for information on our titles

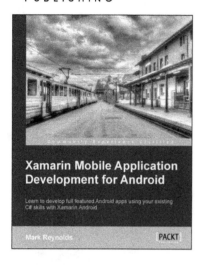

Xamarin Mobile Application Development for Android

ISBN: 978-1-78355-916-9   Paperback: 168 pages

Learn to develop full features Android apps using your existing C# skills with Xamarin Android

1. Gain an understanding of both the Android and Xamarin platforms.

2. Build a working multi-view Android app incrementally throughout the book.

3. Work with device capabilities such as location sensors and the camera.

Ionic Cookbook

ISBN: 978-1-78528-797-8   Paperback: 264 pages

Over 20 exciting recipes to spice up your application development with Ionic

1. Learn how to utilize the robust features of Ionic CLI and its framework to create, develop, and build your mobile app.

2. Explore new integrations with various Backend-as-a-Services, along with AngularJS modules, for creative solutions.

3. Use out-of-the-box Ionic functionalities, customize existing components, and add new components with this comprehensive, step-by-step guide.

Please check **www.PacktPub.com** for information on our titles